Couples
at
the Crossroad

Couples
at
the Crossroad

✦

Finding the Path with a Heart

Dr. Neal L. Wiseman

iUniverse, Inc.
New York Lincoln Shanghai

Couples at the Crossroad
Finding the Path with a Heart

All Rights Reserved © 2004 by Dr. Neal L. Wiseman

No part of this book may be reproduced or transmitted in any form or by any means, graphic, electronic, or mechanical, including photocopying, recording, taping, or by any information storage retrieval system, without the written permission of the publisher.

iUniverse, Inc.

For information address:
iUniverse, Inc.
2021 Pine Lake Road, Suite 100
Lincoln, NE 68512
www.iuniverse.com

ISBN: 0-595-29657-2

Printed in the United States of America

Dedicated with love to Marcy
And, of course, to Rachel and Seth

Contents

Preface xi

Stage I   Contact

CHAPTER 1   First Kiss 3

    The Search 4

    Rapport. 7

    Bonding 8

    Ownership 9

    Burden 9

    Training 10

    Past Performances 11

    The Screening. 11

CHAPTER 2   Compatibility 14

    Intimacy-Passion-Commitment 14

    Motivations for Coupling 17

    Destructive Attitudes and Behaviors 21

    Comfort Zones 23

CHAPTER 3   Voices 29

CHAPTER 4   Toxic Personalities. 37

    The Obsessive Thinker 37

    The Suspicious Thinker 39

    The Non-Thinker. 41

    The Impulsive Thinker 43

    "The Trapper" 45

viii   Couples at the Crossroad

"The Double Binder" 46

The "Intimacy from Ten Feet Away" (IFTFA) Person 46

"The Whiner" 47

"The Armadillo" 47

"The Possessor" 48

Stage II   Connection

CHAPTER 5   Connecting 51

The Seven Signs of Love 52

Intimacy 56

Contact Boundaries 58

Intrusion and Abandonment 59

CHAPTER 6   Commitment 63

CHAPTER 7   The Power of Moods 67

The Anger Sequence 68

The Humiliation Sequence 70

The Failure Sequence. 76

The Addiction Sequence 77

Mood Chains in Real Life 79

The Flow of Emotions. 82

Mood Duration and Quality 82

Uniqueness of Mood Sequences. 82

Disruption of Mood Phases 83

Feelings of Well-being 84

Feelings Don't Last Forever 84

Emotional Death 85

Acts of Destruction 85

Feelings of Confusion 86

CHAPTER 8   Assuming Control 87

CHAPTER 9   Scripts Lovers Live 94

Early Decisions 95

Life Script Heroes 97

The Don'ts and the Do's. 97

Life Script Exercises. 101

Stage III   Secret Fears, Secret Desires

CHAPTER 10   Hidden Realities 107

Courage 107

Moments of Truth 108

The Paradox of Change. 109

The Nature of Awareness 110

CHAPTER 11   Exercises in Awareness. 114

Exercise 1: The Three Spheres. 114

Exercise 2: Becoming You Becoming Me 116

Exercise 3: Contact/Withdrawal 117

Exercise 4: Create-A-Product 119

Exercise 5: Finger-Pointing. 122

Exercise 6: Yes/No 124

Exercise 7: Have To/Choose To 127

Exercise 8: Fears/Wishes 130

Exercise 9: Make-A-Sandwich. 133

Exercise 10: Expanding Your Boundaries 135

CHAPTER 12   Dream Come True 137

A Leg 137

Dreams—Then and Now 139

Dreams as "Unfinished Business" 140

Dreams as Part of the Grieving Process. 142

Dreams as Existential Messages 145

Ann's Dream and Mike's Journey into Intimacy. 148

CHAPTER 13   Final Word 150

APPENDIX A   The Decision Index. 151

x   Couples at the Crossroad

Appendix B   Four Couples at the Crossroad 165

Margaret and Howard 165

Susan and Dennis 169

Angela and Jim 172

Lisa and Billy 175

A Personal Note 179

Index 181

Preface

"Make a sandwich," I said.

"Let me understand, doctor," she responded, "you want me to make a sandwich?"

"Yes, I would like you to make a husband sandwich," I told the now very perplexed woman. "Just imagine that you are placing him between two pieces of bread and taking a bite. See how it tastes, experience the texture, and experience the chewing."

The confused woman did exactly as I asked. After a few minutes, she screwed up her face.

"What's wrong?" I asked.

"This tastes awful. It's stringy and tough and I just can't swallow it."

"How does this relate to your marriage?" I asked.

"It's the same way with my husband. He's really hard to take. I just want to spit him out, the marriage included."

I next heard from the woman about three months later. "I'd like to make an appointment," she told my secretary. "I think I have a lot to talk about."

Over the course of the next several months, we worked on several issues related to disappointment, anger, grieving, and "shame." Of course, she had already completed the hard work: She had made the decision to leave her husband. (In fairness, I should point out that her husband also "made a sandwich" and found her to be "fatty" and "not at all tasty." Both parties amicably accepted the decision to part.)

To make wise decisions, suggested Carlos Castenada, one of our more colorful anthropologists, we need only look to the "path with a heart." Castenada's advice rings true, but decisions about love relationships are difficult. Learning the "path with a heart" is troublesome for most, and seemingly impossible for others.

Couples at the Crossroad is a book for people who need to answer the vexing question: What do I do next? It's about people whose search for the secret of building a comfortable, durable bridge between themselves and their lovers has finally brought them to a decision point—a crossroad. The crossroad may appear as soon as five minutes after the first meeting, or it may appear fifty years later.

A three-dimensional love evolves through three stages. Each stage brings an opportunity for a successful coupling or for emotional pain. The earliest stage—the stage of the initial contact—requires us to assess only the *probability* of happiness, a seemingly simple process that becomes hellish in nature unless we train ourselves to look beyond the first jolt of excitement. Eliminating losers and picking the real contenders for our affections is the important objective during the first few weeks of contact. Eliminating the losers is relatively easy, but only if we train ourselves to be aware of certain kinds of behaviors and attitudes. Picking winners is far more difficult, but following a few painless rules will at least increase the odds of a good pick.

During the second stage, we connect with our lover at a deeper level. Intimacy, commitment, and communication become the hallmarks of the relationship. However, even here we need to make decisions. Relationships change. New realities supplant the initial lightning bolt of passion, new realities that will either diminish or enhance the likelihood of a durable happiness. Our task during this stage is to discover whether we are compatible with our lover's life style and his deeper personal values.

The third stage marks the point where we actually couple with our partner. We begin to behave, think, and feel as a unit rather than as two separate people. The closeness brings with it other problems: Allowing someone inside us creates sensitivities and feelings of intrusion or abandonment. We often suppress our true feelings for the sake of peace and quiet, only to have them re-emerge at unguarded moments. Yet, the success of the coupling process depends on honesty, and our insight into the fears, wishes, and demands implicit in the relationship.

In *Couples at the Crossroad,* we examine the three stages of love, its three-dimensional quality, its seven signs, and the reasons we choose a particular person to be our partner. We point out the behaviors and the attitudes that destroy relationships, and why people keep trying despite the pain. We explore the life scripts lovers write for themselves. We discuss "toxic" personalities, the roles of chronic failure, anger, and the addictions, and finally the creative power of dreams.

Finally, we put the pieces together, hoping a picture emerges that will lead to the answer of the most important question of all: Is s/he (still) the one for me?

To protect the identities of former patients, the cases presented are in actuality composite pictures of real people with whom I have worked for nearly thirty years. I dramatized certain events and details in order to enhance the readability of the material. I based the extensive dialogue on real conversations. Hundreds of

Preface xiii

couples, families, and people of all ages contributed to the thinking that went into the writing of the book, and to each one I offer my gratitude.

I owe a debt of gratitude to Richard Borofsky and Michael Vincent Miller, Directors of the Boston Gestalt Institute. I would also like to recognize the influence of the writings of Frederick Perls, the "discoverer" of Gestalt Therapy, and my brief but powerful contacts with Ruth Cohn, Founder of the Institute for Living/Learning in New York. The writings of Eric Berne and his protégé, Claude Steiner, inspired the life scripts material. The late Dr. Felix del Vecchio, a psychologist of extraordinary talent, lent his support and critique at crucial times before his sad and untimely death.

I also want to thank those people who set a tone of encouragement: Evelyn and Charles Spencley, Fran and Lee Greb, Amy and Peter Norris, Ferma and Barry Kipnes, Bobbie and Bill Brodie, Myrna and Paul Lubin, Leslie and George Fox, Dr. Sally Maxwell, Steve and Denise Hengeli, Marty Rosen, Paul Farb, Carl Reitman, Dr. Heidi Melius, Dr. Bernard Grzyb, and my colleagues in the Broward County Public Schools.

I hope you enjoy your experience with *Couples at the Crossroad*. The process of coupling can be tricky, but less so when we learn to recognize the "path with a heart."

NW
Ft. Lauderdale
July 27, 2003

Stage I
Contact

1

First Kiss

We meet someone quite extraordinary. We tell our friends, "This is it! This is the person I've been waiting for all my life." Our friends smile and wish us luck.

We continue to date. The courtship is fine: fancy restaurants, flowers, gentle kisses, and tender caresses. After a few months, we still enjoy the attention we give and we get—at least most of the time. However, something is different. We try to understand the minor irritations, the petty arguments, and the differences of opinion. We finally conclude that maybe this isn't the person for whom we've been waiting all our lives.

Sometimes we are certain about who will make us happy, and sometimes we are not. If we happen to stumble upon the right person, no problem: We enjoy the moment, disregard any conflicting realities, and make plans for the future. If our selection definitely is not the right one, again there is no problem. We simply find a way to let him know, accept the disappointment, attempt to part as friends, and learn from the experience.

Sometimes, however, even when we intuitively know the relationship is not going anywhere, we refuse to give up; we make excuses and we procrastinate, hoping things will change.

How can we be sure? After all, we have only known each other for a few days (months, years). In addition, he has become part of our lives: The smell of him, the taste of him, the small gifts and remembrances, the chuckles at an "inside" joke, the smiles at an understanding secret to the outside world. All the tiny things tug and pull at our waking thoughts like toddlers wanting attention. To rid ourselves of this person now would leave us emptier than we were before. A hole exists where our heart once was.

For most of us, the initial contact with a potential mate involves hedonistic pleasure and the excitement of the senses. We become fascinated (fasten-ated). A certain look, the sound of the voice, the agility of a movement, the touch of the skin, the taste of the lips, the smell of the hair become a complex package of sen-

4   Couples at the Crossroad

sations that lead most often to an overwhelming feeling of sexiness. When this feeling develops into a "caring," expressed as unselfish giving mixed with the full acceptance of pleasure, we are well on our way to "love," the feeling that transcends the senses and knocks at the door of a mature sense of intimacy, commitment, and passion.

We often experience the contact stage as "madness." (During the middle ages, marrying because of "love" was outlawed for noblemen whose judgment might become so impaired that the family wealth was at risk.) The primary feeling is infatuation, commonly a one-way affair that requires no real love-partner. The object of our attention smites us with a smile; we consume him with our entire being. There is no reality during this phase of t(w)ogetherness. Our lover is a fantasy; he doesn't exist in actuality, but we refuse to believe it. Often the object of our desires has no idea that he has precipitated a state of excitement so overwhelming that his mere presence keeps our loins and minds boiling over in erotic fantasies and happily-ever-after endings.

Life becomes less complicated for us once we learn to separate the wheat from the chaff. Is this the right person for me? Are we compatible? Will the relationship last? Should we invest our time and energy trying to make this relationship work? Many questions but one goal: to separate the wheat from the chaff.

The Search

The search for an effective way to help couples make wise decisions about their relationships began in February 1981. Most people had been stranded in their homes on this particular day, and I had not expected anyone to keep his therapy appointment. An unexpected blizzard had swept through Boston leaving behind it a two and a half-foot blanket of snow. The wind chill factor knocked the temperature down into the single digits. Nonetheless, at precisely 10:00 AM, my secretary buzzed to tell me that the new couple had arrived.

The office door opened and in walked an attractive man and woman, each one I judged to be in the mid thirties. Ann was a tall, impeccably dressed blond-haired woman. Mike, speaking with a crisp British accent, was well over six feet in height, handsome, polished in his manner, and eager to talk.

And so began a dozen counseling sessions, Ann and Mike telling me they were at a "crossroad," and that they needed to make a decision about their respective futures.

"We're in love," they assured me. "We do not really know what the problem is, but it needs to be resolved quickly," Ann said within the first ten minutes of the session. We were to spend several months tracking down the problems, the doubts, the fears, and the insecurities, and in the process, Ann and Mike learned all about who they were and what they wanted from each other.

About six months before, Ann had gone to England to present a paper at a writer's conference. As a writer, she was interested in the plight of mature women who had similar marital experiences. The paper she presented discussed the changing language of romance, the use of specific "romantic" words to stimulate and provoke feelings and thoughts. Her paper scored a hit with the audience.

After the applause had subsided, Mike approached her. He had come to hear her speak because even in London, where he was then living, he had read her books and thought she had a wonderful sense of humor. He had owed it to himself to meet her at this conference. Had he known how beautiful she was, he told her, he would have thought of some way of meeting her even earlier.

At first, Ann couldn't accept Mike's flattery. It felt uncomfortable, she said, "rather like an ill-fitting suit." She had to admit, though, that Mike's attention did stir up old memories and feelings she had buried after her divorce two years before. She also had to admit that these stirrings scared her to death: She wanted to run, to get away quickly before—and she knew it would happen—the man's flattery dissolved the defenses she had worked so hard to erect.

After her second divorce, Ann had abandoned the search for male companionship, investing her energies instead in her family and her work. She had reconciled herself to a life of celibacy and service. Now her resolve was melting, and she was rediscovering the feelings of passion and desire she had suppressed long ago. Here with this man, with this stranger, she suddenly felt weak and vulnerable. She was confused, powerless, and worst of all, she knew that if he had asked her to extend her visit, she would have done so without hesitation.

The truth was that Ann and Mike had been searching for the right combination of passion, intimacy, and commitment for years. They had begun the search for happiness even before their divorces were finalized.

Our first session took place after the couple had been dating for about six months. They wanted to know whether there was away to "make sure that their love would last." There was of course no way to guarantee the durability of their relationship. Still, they needed to learn what couplehood was all about, and we set out to do exactly that.

Ann and Mike had made it through the first of the three stages of coupling. Most people do not. The contact stage may last for minutes or months. However long it lasts, two things are apparent. The first is the intensity of the initial attraction to our prospective mate; the second is the subconscious attempt to get a feel

6   Couples at the Crossroad

for the probability of a successful coupling. The first task involves hormonal chemistry that adds a sense of urgency. The second task is more difficult because the overwhelming sense of sexiness and a longing to find a mate distorts our perception of reality.

When both members of the couple become equally fascinated, fantasies beget fantasies. Today they are only teenagers, but tomorrow, with the help of their lover, they will be kings or queens, warriors of great causes, homeowners, mothers, or fathers of 2.3 bright children, and a 50 per cent shareholder in the greatest love affair that ever was. The results of such a *foliè a deux* can be tragic, of course: early marriage for the innocent and the unprepared, along with the attendant burdens of children, creditors, and an early divorce with the accompanying grief, disappointment, and cynicism. In a large number of instances, however, the fantasies contain a grain of truth and reality that continue to grow and—properly nurtured—continue to inspire passion, intimacy and commitment.

By the time Ann and Mike came for couple's counseling, they had been dating for nearly six months. This was costly in terms of time, money, and inconvenience. Mike had been living in England at the time, and he flew to Boston to be with Ann on a monthly basis. As the relationship grew, returning home became increasingly more difficult, Ann often expressing her muted but persistent desire for Mike to remain with her and her children.

Ann and Mike came for couples' counseling because they were frightened. Both had been through bad marriages and unsatisfying relationships for many years. They were convinced, they told me, that they were deeply in love. It pained Mike to leave Ann alone. In fact, he had begun to consider leaving his job and moving to Boston so he could be with Ann and her two sons. However, both recognized that a decision of this magnitude was a "bit crazy," considering they had only known each other for less than a year. What should they do, they wanted to know. Their fears appeared to be rooted in feelings of helplessness and loss of control. Each had spent many years alone, independent, and free to make his own decisions. Now, as a couple, they needed to develop the kind of interdependency each one had until now tried to avoid. They agreed that at times the tension was so great that despite the fact they felt strongly about each other they had considered splitting up. To their credit, they were trying to sort through their feelings, an especially crucial step during the first stage of coupling.

To assist the sorting process, we spent much time talking about the coupling process, its successes, and its failures.

Rapport

The first contact with someone who attracts our interest is special. We are still in a naïve state; our perceptions have not yet become distorted. It is the first and only time we can sense the true essence of the other person. Our lack of experience with the person allows us to judge the situation without the rationalizations and defenses we are apt to erect later on in the relationship after we have invested so much time and energy that we resist making necessary changes.

Rapport, the ability to deepen a relationship over time, is an important factor, but most of us fail to notice. It involves the establishment of flexible boundaries. Some people have boundaries that allow us in; others have boundaries that keep us out. Still others have boundaries that vary in their permeability. Ideally, we want a lover who will welcome us in when we want to make a strong contact, and who will allow us to leave when the contact becomes too strong or uncomfortable.

When intimacy is high and the bonding is optimal, there is a steady deepening of the relationship: We begin to resonate with our lover, we see things the same way, and we respond to humor in a similar fashion. Our lover is a welcome guest who knows when s/he should leave us alone, and who knows when we want her to stay close. During the hormonal "chemistry" phase of a relationship, the relationship actually is stagnant; lust is merely lust, after all (but please do not underestimate its value). With time and experience, however, the relationship—if it follows a more or less normal sequence—changes into an admixture of libidinal energy, plus intimacy, plus commitment. This change is the hallmark of a deepening of the relationship. Each week, each month, becomes a celebration of intimacy; we are able to go deeper into our lover until finally we are able to visit her/his soul. The soul is the place where intimacy, passion, and commitment merge into a single indistinguishable whole. The degree to which we can enter our lover's soul is the essence of love in its truest sense.

We define rapport as the evolving feelings we have towards another person at various points in time. We assess the way we feel at the very beginning, at three months, at six months, at one year, at five years, and at ten years. If the relationship continues to deepen after ten years, there is something very right about it. Please note, however, that just being together for an extended period does not mean much; rapport means that the relationship *deepens* with time. If the relationship fails to deepen, we might need to reassess the nature of our relationship with our lover. Rapport and intimacy are two of the more important variables in any relationship.

Bonding

The quality of intimacy we experience as adults reflects the quality of intimacy we experienced as children, and the quality of intimacy we experience as children depends in large part on the quality of our attachment to parents and other caretakers.

If we carefully observe infants directly after birth, we find that even within the first few hours after delivery, the infant, if placed on the mother's stomach, will crawl upward in search of mother's breast. Mother's willingness to first nourish the infant in the womb and then to nourish the infant *on demand* as it enters the world becomes one of the most important developmental events in a growing child's life, and one of the major ingredients in teaching adults to develop trusting and secure relationships with potential mates and/or lovers.

Among couples where one partner has trouble attaching or connecting to the other, we reliably find distressing personal interactions, anger, rage, cyclical patterns of depression, poor self-esteem, an absence of feelings of safety and security, a lack of trust, and a high demand for personal attention. Deception, lying, and lack of remorse appear regularly among the complaints of couples seeking counseling.

At times, we find a compulsive self-reliance. The attachment disordered partner attempts to avoid feelings of closeness by neither needing nor being needed by others. At other times, we find the opposite—the compulsive search for caring, a search characterized by the urgent, and the frequent need for consolation. Unfortunately, this particular trait also appears in individuals who have a compulsive need to be free from personal responsibility.

We may observe angry withdrawal: The disconnected partner feels that attachment figures are inaccessible. He feels his demands for attention are ignored. Even when the attachment-disordered partner wants to withdraw, the withdrawal has a spiteful, vindictive, and angry quality about it. Clearly, early infant losses affect adult intimacy—the very thing that the distressed partner needs in order to "heal" himself.

Our lover might have a history of a strong normal attachment to his/her parents or primary caretaker, or an abnormally close bonding that might interfere with other relationships. The bonding capacity of other people might be "weak" or nonexistent because of early death/abandonment of parents or a lack of proper care as an infant. The ability to bond quickly and deeply often reveals itself within the first few minutes of meeting someone. If we feel a strong initial contact that fails to deepen with time, the chances are this pattern will continue throughout the relationship. The capacity for strong attachments is essential for intimacy in a relationship; it is less essential for the high passion/low-commitment/low intimacy love relationship.

Ownership

We should not overlook the concept of being "owned" by a problem or by life circumstances. Many are the unhappy wives who complain of husbands whose work keeps them from attending the mundane business of home life. Moreover, many are the husbands who complain of a wife who is consumed and "owned" by the next sale or the next make-up fad that costs a bundle and, aside from a more made-up, more expensively clothed woman, provides few other benefits. The worst case study is the person who is "owned" by an addiction or a chronic medical problem that consumes time, energy, money, and eventually hope. However, if we love someone, what can we do? We want to be there for him, to take care of him, and to give him our strength. It is a very difficult choice to make. We should be aware however that when we couple with someone whose problems own him, that problem also owns us.

Burden

Burden denotes any situation or condition that taxes the mind/body: medical problems, financial concerns, unemployment, overwork, losses (death, job, family, and incarceration), poor peer relationships, dramatic life changes, concerns about children, marital problems, addictions, etc. The concept of Burden is extremely important: People generally return to a pre-morbid level of functioning when stresses are relieved. If, however, the pre-morbid level of stress is also unmanageable, you can expect continued stress, crisis, and emotional pain. The matter becomes clearer as we go through the exercise of studying our lover's past performance in his relationships with parents, peers, and previous lovers. If the information we need to make a decision is lacking, we might end up playing a longer shot then we had planned.

How do we know when a person is over-burdened? There are signs:

He will demonstrate a variety of bodily symptoms. Each symptom reflects a change in life style, a change in stress level, and a change in his need to express outwardly what has been eating away at her/him inwardly. There may be a change in appetite, and a corresponding change in weight. Diarrhea or constipation dramatically mirrors the need to "let loose" or to "hold back." Back pain,

10   Couples at the Crossroad

headache, neck pain, and stomach pain reflect a failure to end the pain of the relationship. Stuttering, shoulder tension, and teeth grinding serve to prevent the direct expression of anger and rage. Heart pounding, increased blood pressure and hyper-vigilance emphasize the need for fight or flight.

Anxiety, fear, and depression dominate mood. The message behind his frequent decrease in sex drive and apathy is insecurity. Loss of control, anger, frustration, and hopelessness occur all too often. Sleeplessness, emotional sensitivity, uncommunicativeness, and fatigue are the symptoms that most physicians hear about when the over-burdened lover schedules his next physical examination.

Whatever he expresses as bodily and emotional symptoms, he also shows intellectually. His thinking is fuzzy, disorganized, forgetful, and lacking in vigilance. His body's lack of harmony is evident: concentration is poor, speech is pressured, and judgment becomes impaired.

Finally, our over-burdened lover experiences abrupt changes in habits: His exercise regimen decreases along with his ability to relax. Sugar and fat intake and the use of drugs (smoking, alcohol) increase. Irritability, querulousness, and discouragement become the bases for relationships at home and often at work.

Training

An infant's experiences with his caretakers during the first few months will determine his perception of the world, and will influence his response to intimacy. The process of attaching himself to caretakers takes place unconsciously, but its effects are far reaching. Any disruption in the attachment process alters the infant's perception of his world. The results are entirely predictable: Infants raised in a loving environment feel secure in their love relationships. He develops a positive self-regard, feelings of esteem, compassion, and sensitivity. On the other hand, infants whose attachment has been damaged for any one of a number of reasons (e.g., abuse, neglect, the lack of adequate parenting, emotional withdrawal of his caretaker, parent's alcohol or drug abuse, emotional illness, or severe loss) develop insecure attachments and learn to view the world as an emotionally cold and hostile place. All dimensions of development are affected—physical, emotional, social, and moral. These early (preverbal) perceptions and accompanying attitudes and behavior persist through adulthood.

Past Performances

Our lover's past performance plays an important role in our attempt to separate the wheat from the chaff. He might have had many relationships in the past, but how many times has he demonstrated the kind of commitment, intimacy, and passion, which in our view, was essential for an enduring relationship. In most cases, what our lover has done in the past will reflect what s/he will do in the future. I remember one couple whose wedding had been canceled no fewer than five times. Why? In each instance, Mr. X had literally left the future Mrs. X at the altar, and Ms. X refused to acknowledge his immaturity and his lack of commitment. Nor did she acknowledge her own culpability in her decision to "try one more time." Both people had a history of failed relationships and apparently were doing everything in their power to maintain that record.

However, past performances do not always predict what will happen in future relationships. For example, a man has had three prior relationships and, in each instance, he decided to terminate the relationship early. Assuming that these relationships did not work out because of completely rational reasons (e.g., lack of compatible life styles, too much burden, or lack of bonding on the part of his previous partner), there is every reason to believe that he might make a very desirable mate for the right woman. Once he gains insight into the nature of his earlier efforts and he has dealt effectively with the difficulties, he may be ready for the affection, intimacy, and commitment for which he has been searching. Under these circumstances, a lover's past performance in and of itself might reveal the *potential* for problems, but does not necessarily portend failure.

The Screening

I asked Ann and Mike to complete several scales I had prepared to measure rapport, ownership, bonding, burden, training, and destructive attitudes (please see Appendix A for samples of the scales). The first consideration was rapport—the ability to deepen the relationship with time. A measure of one's capacity for intimacy, rapport often develops within the first twenty or thirty minutes of meeting someone. We classify rapport as deep, moderate, mild, or absent. The absence of rapport, even after a short period, spells trouble for the future, unless, of course, the parties mean to side-step meaningful involvement.

Ann and Mike developed a deep and abiding rapport almost immediately. They discovered mutual interests and shared a sexiness that neither could ignore. More importantly, the relationship continued to grow. Even now, after six months, they sensed that their emotional closeness deepened every day they spent with each other. Had they discovered that their rapport had not deepened appreciably, it would have meant that their acts of "intimacy" were really acts of deception. Shallowness of feeling and evolving rapport appear to be antagonistic processes.

While Ann found nothing in Mike's past to suggest a problem in that area, Mike was not entirely convinced that Ann did not have a problem with "ownership." He pointed out that her writing consumed her, and further that she had had a history of taking medication for various emotional problems. This led to a discussion of how Ann was going to manage without her antidepressant medication and other mood altering supplements. Ann's response: "I haven't been on any medication since we've been dating! I do take St. John's Wort, but I know it's just a placebo. As far as my writing goes, it doesn't own me, but it does ride me hard…"

We discussed the "Burden" each person carried around with him. Neither Ann nor Mike expressed any concern in this area. While both had experienced a bit of stress in recent months, the stress was very manageable.

Likewise, caring, albeit occasionally rigid, parents had raised each of them. There was no evidence of any real "trainer" problems, nor was there any evidence of a significant problem with bonding and rapport. We examined these issues in detail. Ann's attachment with her parents seemed to be close, but not abnormally so. Mike's attachment, on the contrary, had been slightly too loose. Each had adjusted reasonably well—certainly well enough to accommodate a healthy relationship.

We also discussed each person's past relationships. Ann had been married two times. Mike had been married one time, but he had been engaged several times. The discussion of this topic centered on the reason why the previous relationships had not worked out. Mike admitted he had a tendency to involve himself with women so burdened with problems that he became overwhelmed. In each case, he decided the only way out of the dilemma was to make a hasty retreat before a permanent state of unhappiness supplanted the one-time joyous relationships.

Ann found it hard to be objective about her previous relationships. She had married two men, both of whom appeared to be highly dependent on her. The reasons for her divorces in both cases revolved about the possessiveness and lack of respect from her ex-husbands. At the time, she became so depressed that she sought psychiatric care. After several months of therapy and a modest course of medication, she decided to head out on her own. She had maintained a cordial relationship with both men, especially the father of her two sons. As she laid the

First Kiss 13

reasons for her two divorces before Mike, it became clear that her reasons for the divorces were sound. Of course, the real question was why she made two bad decisions in the first place. Whatever the reason, she and Mike were sure that they based their decisions on a growing awareness of their mutual needs, mutual respect, and mutual desire.

2

Compatibility

After the first of a dozen sessions, it became increasingly clear that Ann and Mike had a lot more to deal with than just indecisiveness. Their unsuccessful marriages had left them wondering whether they were capable of being "compatible" with *anybody*, let alone their respective ex-mates.

Are couples in love necessarily compatible?

The answer is, "It depends."

Intimacy-Passion-Commitment

We tend to (con)fuse "love" with a momentary passion, an intense experience of intimacy, or a vow of commitment. Love, however, is three-dimensional; while we perceive any one of the three dimensions, in its pure state, as "love," rarely does a relationship develop into a durable and satisfying coupling without the qualities of all three dimensions. The intimacy-passion-commitment triad produces many combinations, and some combinations tend to produce greater happiness than others do.

Those of us who value intimacy enjoy a best-friend relationship with our lover. We share interests, hobbies, pastimes, religion, and perhaps politics. We tend to be thoughtful and gentle, caring and nurturing, and equal partners. These are traits that we hold dearer than the sizzling passion so often described in romance novels. We reveal ourselves slowly and gradually.

The passion dimension, on the other hand, is intense and often short-lived. Devotion alternates with jealousy and insecurity; emotional peaks and valleys occur with regularity. We may believe in love at first sight and experience high sexual energy, but we often need reassurance, despite our lover's declarations of love and adoration. We also crave excitement and value our lover's physical attributes (beauty, strength, agility) over intelligence. As high-passion couples, we also tend to disclose inner drives, fears, desires, and strivings soon after our first

14

contact with our lover. Plans for the future are short term, reflecting our tendency to be impulsive and capricious.

A high-commitment relationship generally values self-sacrifice, forgiveness of transgressions, and consistent support during times of adversity. Planning includes long-range goals, and our relationship emphasizes patience and "being there" rather than passion or self-disclosure.

Because Mike and Ann had already known each other for several months, I handed them the *3-D Compatibility Scale* at the end of our second session (you will find the complete scale in Item #7 on the Decision Index in Appendix A). Their responses to this brief test revealed feelings and attitudes that neither one could have appreciated before the start of their search for the "path with a heart." Before examining Ann's and Mike's answers, let's look at several common variations of compatibility as defined by the passion-intimacy-commitment triad:

Profile I: Two highly committed people displaying at least average passion and average intimacy appear to be "compatible" because their commitment assures consistency and availability.

Profile II: One of the combinations that seems to work out best includes two high passion people who are willing to commit themselves even though one of them has only "average" intimacy. High sexual energy, the desire to be with her lover, and the willingness to endure hardships make this a winning combination. However, the relative lack of self-revelation, as indicated by an average score on the Intimacy scale, will leave the other always wondering, "What is s/he really thinking?"

Profile III: Another desirable combination pairs a high intimacy, high-commitment wo/man with a high intimacy, high-commitment wo/man. Nurturing feelings toward her lover and a commitment for life are more important than passion, excitement, or sexual contact. The couple shares thoughts, interests, and a strong friendship as well as a strong desire to be with each other. The passion dimension should fall within the average range; otherwise, the relationship may suffer from a lack of excitement and/or interest.

Profile IV: An unusual but not uncommon combination features high energy, satisfying sexual contact, romance, and a willingness to endure adversity, at least by one of the parties. One of members of the couple is high in passion and commitment, and average in intimacy. The other member of the pair is high in passion and intimacy, and average in commitment. The first person will always wonder what his/her partner is thinking, but s/he also knows his lover will be there when s/he need him. Perhaps more importantly, he knows he can share his thoughts and feelings without criticism.

16   Couples at the Crossroad

Profile V: The longest shot of all consists of a person who scores low on all three dimensions of love matched with a person who scores high on all three dimensions of love. The basis for a satisfying, fulfilling relationship simply does not exist. There will be much tension, stress, confusion, frustration, and emotional withdrawal and a persistent yearning to escape from your partner. Note, however, that during times of adversity (war, famine) couples who have nothing whatever in common get married or cohabitate, and, with time and goodwill, they adapt.

Profile VI: Nothing in Profile VI suggests a potential for happiness: An individual with low passion, low-commitment and high intimacy meets his or her opposite—the individual with high passion, high-commitment, and low intimacy. One partner would dampen the considerable passion of the other, and there would not be enough intimacy and friendship to take the sting out of the constant tension and frustration. One of the member's of the relationship would always be worried about either abandonment or affairs outside the relationship.

Profile VII: This combination of incompatible traits features a high sense of commitment in both parties, but passion and intimacy are extremely low in one and very high in the other. Not only would there be sexual frustration and a yearning for caring and friendship on the part of one partner or the other, but worst of all, the high degree of commitment on both sides would prevent or delay the "cure," namely, to say good-bye and (re)search for the correct path.

Profile VIII: High passion, low-commitment, and low intimacy in both parties characterize the final combination of incompatible traits. This is a wonderful combination for a couple interested in a torrid love affair and a series of one-night stands. The high sexual energy, the romance, the euphoria during the early phases of the relationship all make this the kind of experience people would want on a cruise ship rather than one to be sanctified on the altar. After the first few months, both will want to bow out of the relationship to search for someone else who fits an exciting-but-aloof-and-unstable profile.

Couples who seem to be compatible but who continue to have problems with their relationship need to check out other issues. Differences in background and values, the motivation for coupling, personality styles, and destructive life scripts, and the lack of awareness are among the most probable problem areas. We address these factors in later sections.

Ann and Mike completed their 3-D Compatibility Scales with the following results:

Ann's compatibility profile suggested she was high on all three dimensions.

Mike's ratings indicated that he perceived himself as high in Passion, average in Intimacy, and high in Commitment.

Ann appeared to be the partner who was most willing to reveal herself. On the other hand, she perceived Mike as a highly passionate man who could commit himself to the relationship and enjoy—at least to an average degree—emotional closeness. This was not totally out of line with Mike's own ratings. The only fly in the proverbial ointment was Mike's average level of intimacy. Considering Mike's life script—his father's insistence that logic and intelligence were of greater import than emotional freedom—it wasn't too hard to see why Mike might have had trouble exhibiting intimacy.

At the end of the exercise, Ann asked the unanswered question: "Are we compatible?"

If the profiles were accurate, I told her, it appeared that she and Mike would get along quite nicely under most circumstances. Making love would be satisfying and she would never have to worry about Mike's commitment to her or her children. I also noted, however, that she if demanded that Mike share his *inner* experiences—intimate thoughts and feelings—he might find it very difficult.

So the answer to Ann's question was, "Yes, you are compatible, but..." I tried to soften the response by observing that the odds favored a good marriage, if that was the route they chose, as long as they recognized the potential problem and were prepared to deal with it.

They wanted a different answer. They needed more reassurance, and they continued their search.

Motivations for Coupling

If you ask ten of your dearest single friends why they want to get married, you'll probably get ten different answers, but the chances are that most of the answers will involve the notion of "love." Love, however, is a relatively new phenomenon as far as coupling is concerned.

Early psychoanalysts told us that the act of coupling might reflect any of the following: the universal fear of loneliness, chemical attraction, electricity, magnetism, unconscious mate prototypes, toxic and diseased brains, odors that attract perspective mates, archetypal genes in the male and geographic proximity. Notably absent from each of these processes is the free-will version of love, presumably the dominant reason for coupling—at least in the industrial nations.

When we couple with another human being, the event defines itself on one side by a commonly unspoken agreement about the exclusiveness of the relationship, and, on the other side, by a wedding celebration, cohabitation, or some other public declaration about our commitment. At this point, we demonstrate the exclusivity of our relationship through "couple" behaviors. In short, we agree to abide by the social rules and mores governing coupled relationships.

Coupling, at any level, is a response to our mutual needs and desires: physical attraction, availability, vitality, energy level, ability to communicate verbally and nonverbally, style of life, intelligence, humor, wisdom, affection and warmth, sexual attraction, personal values, passion, intimacy, and the capacity for commitment. The specific ingredients making up the needs-and-desires smorgasbord vary according to the emotional/social/financial profiles of each person in the relationship. Wishes and fears unique to each person make up these profiles.

With time and experience, each couple develops a unique character that is qualitatively different from the individual traits of singleness contributed by either partner. The amalgamation marks a change in the very nature of the relationship.

One plus one equals more than two when we are involved with others. The admixture of our joint talents, desires, needs, and values is different from what we would exhibit as separate individuals.

Two "weak" characters can produce a "strong" bonding and an enduring relationship. On the other hand, we often find that two "strong" characters can produce a flawed and tenuous coupling.

Some relationships simply are more successful than others are. When we examine the elements of successful marriages, we often find the following:

1. The ability of each partner to stand alone if necessary: While each person supports the other in the relationship, neither person is completely dependent on the other. Completely dependent people become "enmeshed" in their relationships. Their boundaries become "loose" and ill defined. One person becomes the other; they see the world through the same eyes. Perceptions of reality become blurred and idiosyncratic. Rather than roaming freely in each other's life space, each unwittingly becomes trapped behind a lover's boundary and cannot find the way out. We speak of this as "confluence"—the merging of ourselves with our environment. Separate identities no longer exist: Everybody becomes a "we," an unhealthy situation to be sure—especially when the "we" includes at least one partner who is addictive or abusive. This atmosphere produces a co-dependency and, in the worst case study, co-paranoia, a *folie à deux*, where both parties become partners in the worst crime there is—the destruction of the self.

2. The ability of each person to benefit from the union: Each half of the couple enriches the social and emotional life of the other half, and in turn becomes more self-actualized than it would be if the other person did not exist. The high divorce rate gives testimony to the fact that marriages often fail this simple test of viability: At least one of the partners feels that he isn't fully ripening or benefiting from the relationship. There may be other benefits—security, acceptance by peers and parents, etc., but the essence of life—excitement and growth—is missing.

3. The "Resonance Factor": Each person in a relationship "resonates" at a certain energy level. Like violin strings, two people "vibrating," each one at a slightly different energy level, influences the other and combines with him so that a synergy is developed. The synergy results in an emotional, sexual, and intellectual harmony that produces a more vibrant, stronger, and more beautiful "chord." The violinist properly playing two strings at the same time produces a sound that is superior to either string played singly. In the same sense, two "weak" partners can often be part of a synergistic relationship that results in a strength and harmony.

These three qualities produce stability, symmetry, and stamina in the relationship—qualities that often elude individuals on their own. They also enable couples to smooth out emotional hills and valleys—the occasional imbalances that every relationship must endure.

Whether we like to admit it or not, each of us carries a shopping list of ingredients while searching for our soul mate. Some ingredients are obvious: geographical compatibility, similarity of background and values, physical attraction (height, weight and "prettiness"), age, religion, occupation, intelligence, creativity, and lifestyle.

For the romantic couple, there really is only one path to follow when deciding whom to choose as a mate. As Carlos Casteneda has advised:

"Look at every path closely and deliberately, then ask yourselves a crucial question: 'Does this path have a heart?' If it does, the path is good; if it doesn't, it is of no use."

In reality, however, there are sometimes not-so-readily admitted reasons why we choose to become part of someone's life: immigrants desiring citizenship, a parent who wants a mother/father for his children, young wo/men who want someone to take care of them, money, and wealth, social status...the list goes on.

The question of motivation played a vital role in Ann's relationship with Mike. They were happy with each other, but they worried about whether their motivations for becoming a couple were compatible. Ann wanted someone who could share her love of literature, someone who could show passion, and mostly, she said, she wanted someone who would stand by her side no matter what. For his part, Mike wanted a woman who could analyze life events dispassionately when necessary, share his interest in politics, and someone who could be a good mother.

By the end of the session, it became clear that each individual really was different. They were discouraged. Could they possibly overcome their differences? Were their motives for getting into a relationship so different that it would not work out for them? It was time for a more objective approach to the issues surrounding the motivation for coupling. I gave each one a scale entitled simply, *Reasons for Coupling* and asked them to bring back the completed forms the following week. (Please see item #9 in Appendix A for a sample of the Reasons for Coupling Scale).

When we next met, Ann told me that she and Mike had agreed on a dozen reasons for being together. Passion, intimacy, friendship, and sexual attraction were very important and each believed the other party felt the same way. For Ann, having mutual interests, feeling needed, financial security, having someone care for her, and having a father for her two sons were also very important. Mike and Ann rated humor high on the list of motivations. The one area that seemed to bother them was "Commitment." Ann scored her commitment as Very Important and perceived that it was not nearly as important for Mike. For his part, Mike rated Commitment "Important" for both of them, noting that Ann had often said that she did not need marriage or a diamond ring to legitimatize the relationship. This difference in their ratings led to a discussion about "mixed messages" and honest communication. When asked to answer the questions at the end of the rating scale, neither had trouble: Both agreed that their ability to be intimate at every level was the crucial ingredient in the relationship, and they agreed that the risk of their relationship failing was minor.

Our discussions revealed that each person had his own reasons for seeking out a partner. For Ann, romance and passion mixed with security and humor were the most important considerations. For Mike, finding someone with whom he felt secure was most important. He also liked the idea that he had discovered a partner who would be open to new experiences. Ann and Mike had satisfied themselves that their motivations for coupling were compatible.

Destructive Attitudes and Behaviors

We need to be particularly aware of blatantly destructive habits, attitudes, and behaviors during the dating stage. We often see destructive behaviors in men and women who have trouble bonding, establishing rapport, and who have been raised in highly critical or impersonal settings. You'll find a scale to measure Destructive Behavior and Attitudes in the Appendix (Item #6 on the Decision Index in Appendix A). The scale describes 25 troublesome behaviors and attitudes that play havoc with relationships. Among these potential problems are disagreements over money, sex, politics, values, emotional and physical abuse, and the addictions.

Serious disagreements and abusive behaviors magnify the flaws in the coupling process. This is especially true during Stage I as each member of the couple is trying to adapt to the other's life style. For example, the alcoholic may begin to drink a little more than before, waiting to see how we will react. An early and definitive rejection might drive him to AA, to a psychotherapist, or to sobriety. A clear acceptance of the drinking will encourage more of the same in future years, a path appealing to some but not many. The same scenario applies to the gambler, the rage-aholic, the clingy person, or the depressed one. Our choices are limited: We can accept, reject, or simply ignore the behavior. Accepting and ignoring the destructive behavior will soon lead to despair and desperation.

I introduced Ann and Mike to the Destructive Behavior and Attitude Scale below (see Item #6 on the Decision Index in Appendix A) and asked them to complete it before the next session. Here is how the two people responded to the items. The "A" corresponds to Ann's ratings; the "M" corresponds to the way Mike rated the item.

	Destructiveness Scale			
	Not Damaging		**Mildly Damaging**	**Very Damaging**
Behavior	*1*	*2*	*3*	*4*
1. Disagreement over $	A, M	___	___	___
2. Gambling	A, M	___	___	___
3. Absence from Home	___	A	M	___
4. Initiation of Sex	A, M	___	___	___
5. Frequency of Sex	A, M	___	___	___

22   Couples at the Crossroad

| | Destructiveness Scale | | |
Behavior	Not Damaging	Mildly Damaging		Very Damaging
	1	2	3	4
6. Quality of Sex	A, M	___	___	___
7. Unfaithfulness	A, M	___	___	___
8. Jealousy	M	A	___	___
9. Impotence/Frigidity	A, M	___	___	___
10. Alcohol/Drug Abuse	___	A	M	___
11. Temper Outbursts	A	M	___	___
12. Physical Abuse	A, M	___	___	___
13. Nagging	A	M	___	___
14. Poor communication	___	M	A	___
15. Dependency/Parents	A, M	___	___	___
16. In-laws	A, M	___	___	___
17. No Mutual Interests	A, M	___	___	___
18. Selfishness	A, M	___	___	___
19. Clinginess	A	___	M	___
20. Lack of Friends	A, M	___	___	___
21. Child-Rearing Values	A, M	___	___	___
22. Different Religions	A, M	___	___	___
23. Lack of Trust	A, M	___	___	___
24. Lack of Respect	A, M	___	___	___
25. Political Differences	___	___	A, M	___

With the exception of item 25, Political Differences, neither Ann nor Mike could think of behaviors or attitudes that they both considered Damaging to their relationship. Both endorsed item #25 because of their philosophical differences. Mike was much more reserved: He could not support "Liberal" issues, such as Affirmative Action and world trade agreements. Ann was a staunch supporter of the ERA and women's rights. While they argued about ERA and the

Civil Liberties Union, they also had learned how to kiss and make up, one of the more difficult skills in relationships. Each respected the other's emotional and physical space. Money was not a concern; child-rearing practices were a concern, but not a major one. None of ratings on the twenty-five items of the scale—with the possible exception of political differences—disclosed behaviors and attitudes so damaging as to threaten the viability of the relationship.

Ann and Mike had always managed to go to bed without any lingering anger toward the other. Had they endorsed three or more "Very Damaging" items or five or more "Somewhat Damaging" items, their relationship would be too painful to endure, and the likelihood of their staying together would have been remote. The wind-chill factor in such cases produces an emotional climate cold enough to cause emotional frostbite. Every day—every hour of every day—tens of thousands of couples assault each other emotionally and physically. Many of the relationships endure despite this, but the price is extremely high: physical and emotional depression, bitterness, belligerence, fear, escapist fantasies, and vindictiveness. Perhaps therapists first developed marriage counseling to combat these feelings, and perhaps it is the reason why it so often fails.

Comfort Zones

Most of us can adapt to an occasional "chilly" day in our relationships. For most of us, however, adjusting to a cold emotional climate is extremely difficult, and we unconsciously (and, sometimes, not so unconsciously) experience a nagging doubt—a quiet irritation—about the viability of the relationship that no amount of adjusting will relieve.

The emotional climate of a relationship refers to the degree to which we feel comfortable with our lover—the degree to which we can tolerate the flat notes of the relationship. Emotional climates can be extreme: relationships can be too "cold" or too "hot." But, then again, people differ in their ability to tolerate extremes. Eskimos adapt nicely to extreme cold; nomads of the desert learn to tolerate the extreme heat of the day with the extreme cold of the night.

Just as weather consists of wind, rain, and low and high pressure systems, the emotional climate of our relationships consists of a flow of behavioral pressures between our lover and us. Many of the behaviors are too subtle to define in everyday terms. Changes in mood, faint changes in body posture and facial gestures, and changes in energy levels contribute to the subtlety of these behaviors. We do not have a vocabulary to describe these changes, but we can feel them, just as we can sense the flat note in an aria. Too many disturbing emotional reactions make

24   Couples at the Crossroad

the climate inhospitable and uncomfortable. On the other hand, even the harshest emotional climates can offer varying degrees of emotional comfort depending on our emotional needs.

Ann and Mike wanted to know whether they matched each other's personality profile. Each one had checked off a laundry list of "Is s/he or isn't s/he?" or "Does s/he or doesn't s/he?" type of questions. Quietly, they tested each other's perception of the world. Was Mike too (in)tense? Or, was he a bit too casual? Would Ann be too dependent, or would her behavior fall within the emotional comfort zones that Mike had established years before? By the time, they would complete their assessments, they would have established personal profiles revealing—all things being equal—whether they could fit comfortably into each other's life. The goal was to help them appreciate emotional "comfort zones."

To help Ann and Mike understand the nature of emotional climates, I asked each of them to complete the Emotional Climate Scale (Item #10 on the Decision Index in Appendix A), thinking that it would sharpen their sensitivity to "flat notes" in the relationship.

Here are the scale and the instructions:

Emotional Climate Scale

Name: _____ Age: _____ Date: _____
Address: _____
City: _____ State: _____ Zip Code: _____
Telephone #s: _____ Email Address: _____
Reason for concern? _____

The 16 items on the scale below comprise a "thermometer" that measures the climate of your relationship. It asks you to judge how much of each personality or physical trait your partner exhibits at any particular time, and how much of each trait you find acceptable. There are two steps to the exercise:

Step 1: Place an "X" at the point on each scale that best describes how your partner behaves or presents himself.

Step 2: Underline an acceptable range for each characteristic. For example, let's rate three traits:

Emotional		1	2	3	4	5	X6 7	Unflappable
Serious		1	2	3	X4	5	6	7	Carefree
Shy		1	2	3	4	X5	6 7	Assertive

Here we find that the rater's partner is a stable, a *serious*, and a somewhat *shy* person. What she feels most comfortable with, however, is a stable, *carefree*, and somewhat *bold* person. In two out of three cases here, her partner falls outside the "emotional comfort" zone.

Complete the following scales in a similar fashion, and answer the questions that follow in order to assess the "emotional climate" of your relationship.

Scales

Joiner	1	2	3	4	5	6	7	Loner
Relaxed	1	2	3	4	5	6	7	Driven
Impulsive	1	2	3	4	5	6	7	Controlled
Secure	1	2	3	4	5	6	7	Worried
Blunt	1	2	3	4	5	6	7	Sophisticated
Shy	1	2	3	4	5	6	7	Assertive
Self-sufficient	1	2	3	4	5	6	7	Dependent
Trusting	1	2	3	4	5	6	7	Guarded
Practical	1	2	3	4	5	6	7	Capricious
Emotional	1	2	3	4	5	6	7	Unflappable
Earthy	1	2	3	4	5	6	7	Pretentious
Serious	1	2	3	4	5	6	7	Carefree
Lackadaisical	1	2	3	4	5	6	7	Disciplined
Reserved	1	2	3	4	5	6	7	Outgoing
Casual	1	2	3	4	5	6	7	Formal
Unattractive	1	2	3	4	5	6	7	Attractive

After you have completed each item, examine the scales where your partner falls outside the emotional comfort zone. To the left of each scale where you seem to be incompatible, write an "I" (Important), an "N" (Not Important) or a "VI"

26   Couples at the Crossroad

(Very Important) to describe the importance of the particular characteristic. Compare the sum of the items that are rated "I"s and the items rated "VI" with the total number of "N"s. Ideally, the number of "I"s plus "VI"s should be far less than the number of "N"s. If the ratio is greater than 1:1, what are the chances of your relationship surviving periods of difficulty?

Here is the profile that Ann produced:

Joiner	1	2	3	4	5	6 X	7		Loner
Relaxed	1	2	3	4	5	6 X	7		Driven
Impulsive	1	2	3	4 X	5	6	7		Controlled
Secure	1	2	3 X	4	5	6	7		Worried
Blunt	1	2	3	4	5	6 X	7		Sophisticated
Shy	1	2	3	4	5 X	6	7		Assertive
Self-reliant	1	2	3 X	4	5	6	7		Dependent
Trusting	1	2	3	4 X	5	6	7		Guarded
Practical	1	2	3 X	4	5	6	7		Capricious
Emotional	1	2	3	4	5	6	7 X		Unflappable
Earthy	1	2	3	4	5	6 X	7		Pretentious
Serious	1	2	3	4 X	5	6	7		Carefree
Disordered	1	2	3	4	5	6 X	7		Disciplined
Reserved	1	2	3 X	4	5	6	7		Outgoing
Casual	1	2	3	4	5	6 X	7		Formal
Unattractive	1	2	3	4	5	6 X	7		Attractive

Ann's ratings suggested that she and Mike were compatible in most of the areas measured. He tended to be more formal, less social, more practical, and a bit more reserved and conservative than she was. However, she also felt that he was extremely attractive and sexy, secure, sophisticated and self-sufficient, all qualities that she always regarded as essential for a relationship to work. Asked about the differences in their temperament, she summed up her feelings quickly: "That's why we're together…to balance each other." That is why, she added, they wanted to stay together. For her, the emotional climate was perfect.

Mike's ratings were slightly different from Ann's. However, his range of comfort was comparable in most areas. Here is what his profile looked like:

Joiner	1	2	3 X 4	5	6	7	Loner
Relaxed	1	2	3	4	5 X 6	7	Driven
Impulsive	1	2	3 X 4	5	6	7	Controlled
Secure	1	2	3 X 4	5	6	7	Worried
Blunt	1	2	3	4	5	6 X 7	Sophisticated
Shy	1	2	3	4	5	6 X 7	Assertive
Self-reliant	1	2	3 X 4	5	6	7	Dependent
Trusting	1	2 X 3	4	5	6	7	Guarded
Practical	1	2	3	4	5 X 6	7	Capricious
Emotional	1	2	3	4 X 5	6	7	Unflappable
Earthy	1	2	3	4 X 5	6	7	Pretentious
Serious	1	2	3	4	5 X 6	7	Carefree
Disordered	1	2	3	4	5 X 6	7	Disciplined
Reserved	1	2	3	4	5	6 X 7	Outgoing
Casual	1	2	3	4 X 5	6	7	Formal
Unattractive	1	2	3	4	5	6 X 7	Attractive

Mike's ratings on the Emotional Climate Scale pointed up the differences between the two people. Mike felt more comfortable with a reserved, practical-minded, less assertive, more controlled woman. That Ann did not satisfy these conditions was not a problem, however. She was beautiful, sophisticated, ambitious, self-directed, down-to-earth, and totally trusting. The areas where they appeared to be incompatible did not damage the relationship in the least. Ann provided Mike with humor, whimsy, a carefree attitude, spontaneity, and, with her "joiner" orientation, further provided him with an entrée to various social and professional organizations. In short, they complemented or, perhaps more accurately, they completed each other.

The emotional climate of a relationship is affected by many factors: different degrees of intimacy, passion, and commitment, different reasons for involvement, and different personality styles. Each source of incompatibility brings with it its own brand of emotional upheaval and emotional pressure systems, some less tolerable than others.

3

Voices

One of the most important and revealing behaviors we can observe during the first few dates involves the "voice" that our prospective suitor uses to communicate with us. In many ways, the voice reflects levels of *passion,* a factor we need to consider carefully when separating the wheat from the chaff.

Passion is the act of knocking down the doors of life, of squeezing out the juices of this moment, not just in sexual activity but also in all endeavors. It is the streaming of energy from somewhere deep inside us—our souls and the souls of a million ancestors. The passion may come out as a curiosity or wonderment, or an orgasm, or as preachy morality. However, in all cases, it comes out. It is *ex*-pressed rather than *re*-pressed or *sup*-pressed. With this *ex*-pression, there is a sharp and quickly recognized contact with the world outside the skin boundary.

We may do it with great words, like poets; with great concepts, like philosophers; or with great emotions/actions, like actors. However, the act of passion reveals itself, it reflects a sense of immediacy and urgency.

The English language is less subtle than many other languages: Spanish, French, and Italian, for example, are more pleasant to the ear and often use fewer words to describe highly complex ideas. Nowhere is this more clear than in our attempts to describe how "romance," "passion," "intimacy," and "love" are the same and yet somehow different. Our popular literature frequently uses these concepts interchangeably. For our purposes, however, differentiating "passion," one of the three dimensions of what we are calling "love," from the other concepts is essential.

Part of the problem is that the idea of "love" is so comprehensive and vague. The Greek word *agape* refers to love as a Godly state of altruism and self-sacrifice; *philia,* on the other hand, connotes loyalty and brotherly/sisterly love, while the word *eros* suggests sexual desire and longing.

Eros, as its derivative "erotic" indicates, conjures up pictures of uninhibited sex play, seductive wo/men engaged in provocative behavior. The original idea of *eros* however was simply to "desire ardently," and its meaning was quite different from the kind of erotica with which we have come to associate it.

The first use of the word *eros* derived from Plato's myth of androgyny. The myth told that originally man and woman were combined as same sex and opposite sex couples. Each couple—man/man, man/woman and woman/woman—was joined back to back. There were four arms and four legs but a single head with two faces. The God Zeus, in order to subjugate these sets of beings, split each couple down the middle. Each single person was thus incomplete and in order to achieve oneness, s/he had to search out his/her other half. Eros referred to the ardent desire, the profound longing to be complete once again. Sexual union was only one of the many ways by which this could be accomplished.

We use Passion in much the same fashion that Plato used the idea of *eros*: the motivation, the striving, the ardent search for the person and activities that complete us and thus empower us as human beings.

Biology and psychology make up the quality we call passion. Biology produces its energy, but it is only obliquely related to the direction our passion takes. Energy and direction come from different places. Energy is biological; direction is psychological. What concerns us here is the direction of passion. The easiest way to convey the psychological idea of passion to Ann and Mike was to define the path of passion in terms of "voices."

The "voices" are voices we really hear, voices from our past, and voices from the present. They may be sweet or gruff; reasonable, playful, or hardworking; or they may be frightened or angry. Whatever their tone, these voices represent the wishes, the fears, or the spontaneous *oohs*, *aahs*, and gasps of people whose attitudes—and platitudes—we have incorporated into our own thinking and into our everyday demeanor.

Ann and Mike heard many of these voices throughout their courtship. They were both people of passion. Every touch and every kiss, every smile and every word, jolted them into an awareness of the now, the never-ending moment when the world outside would disappear, and intimacy and eroticism began to merge.

Ann told the story of their first meeting. Their contact began as a simple greeting, then became fast and focused. As the evening wore on, they found themselves in a love dance, holding each other close and tight, and their hearts—so Ann said in the words of a writer—began beating in slow syncopation. Throughout this long dance, the voices of passion guided their every move.

The voices of passion reflect different aspects of our personality and may say any or all of the following:

Voice #1: "Whatever you do, I'll still love you." This is the voice of the uncritical, totally accepting parent, whose passion lies in protecting, rescuing, pampering, and assuming responsibility for others.

Voice #2: "No matter what you do, I won't love you." This is the voice of the unaccepting, critical parent whose passion reveals itself in exerting control, making demands, and intimidating others.

Voice #3: "Let's deal just with objective reality because people are too confusing." Here the passion is expressed in the pursuit of an "objective" world, often made up of numbers, computers, and "correct" decisions. There may be excitement and emotion, but feelings generally are not personal.

Voice #4: "I want to play. Won't you please join me?" This is the voice of the socialized, happy-go-lucky, spontaneous child. We find passion in curiosity, enchantment, and in the playful interactions with others.

Voice #5: "I am angry or frightened because (1) you push me around, or (2) you won't give me what I want." This is the voice of discontent, frustration, and deprivation often associated with the internalized critical parent voice. The passion reveals itself in missionary zeal and fighting for great causes, or sometimes just fighting—about anything at all.

Voice #6: "I am frightened/sad/lonely/panicky." This is the voice of the infant who cannot cope with current realities. The voice is a small one, often appearing in our dreams—or nightmares. It says, "I feel so small, weak, and inadequate that I can't deal with big people or big problems." The passion often comes out as art, literature, or in less fortunate situations, a craving for drugs and alcohol. The path of the passion often takes the form of an alliance with someone willing to take care of our needs. In extreme cases, the path leads to a yearning for the safety of an institution (jail, mental hospital, or frequent visits to the family physician).

The voices, in all cases, come from old tapes we have stored on the many shelves of our minds. Sometimes the tapes are scratchy, and sometimes they are clear; but always they are with us, guiding us, telling us whether we are doing what they want us to do, and bringing our behavior in line with society's expectations. In many instances, however, the voices lead us unconsciously to feelings of unhappiness or even to acts of self-destruction.

While passion itself is a rumbling volcano of emotion, the voices of passion are responsible for how we express that emotion. They make up one third of the three dimensional love described in the first chapter. They serve as a cornerstone of the contact/connection/coupling process.

32 Couples at the Crossroad

Only we hear the voices of passion, but others see the behaviors they produce. During the beginning phases of a love relationship, the contact and connection phases, the voice is generally that of the playful child.

We want someone to lift us and twirl us around and around, emotionally and physically; we want to laugh and giggle. We want to become dizzy and lose our balance safely just as we did when we were five or six years old—when we spun ourselves around and around until we became too dizzy to stand erect.

It is Three Little Pigs time. We sing and dance, and play tunes on our mind-flutes. Who's afraid of the Big Bad Wolf? Or involvement? Or commitment? We build our relationship, many of us, with expediency. We cannot bother ourselves at this point in the relationship with worrisome thoughts about the strength of the relationship's foundation. We simply want excitement and companionship. Like the songbird in a tree, we whistle and chirp, hoping that our song is heard and returned by the songster on the next branch. The melody is relatively unimportant; the responsiveness and the harmony, however, are important. They signal acceptance and a willingness to play. We are asking, "I want to play...won't you join me?" What we hope to hear is, "Of course I'll play. You sing so well and you're so pretty."

The playful child's voice is not the only voice we hear. We also hear the voice of fear, uncertainty, and at times even panic. At one point, Ann told Mike she was "frightened and confused"; likewise, Mike revealed to Ann that he did not know what she expected of him. Each was responding to the voice of insecurity and anxiety. It was the voice of their *parents'* own fears about the real world beyond *their* skins. It was the voice they heard when they do not know how to act, or when they were frustrated, and the voice they heard when they were afraid they would be rejected. At the deepest level, it was the voice we all hear when we are afraid we will mess ourselves and no one will like us anymore—the voice that tells us we should feel ashamed.

Rarely do the harsh and demanding critical voices reveal themselves during the initial stages of coupling. This would scare off most potential mates. Nor do we expose our "Let's deal with reality" voice too early because—if we are socially aware people—we have learned this voice not only dampens the excitement of the first contact, it does something worse: It "bores" other people, that is, it digs too sharply into the relationship. The seriousness of the voice becomes intrusive and invokes a something less than playful response.

Most of us reserve our critical voice or our angry voice for special occasions:

Voices   33

1. The angry voice is designed to establish boundaries; it is a way of saying to someone, "Stay out or there will be a price to pay!"

2. We also use the critical voice sadistically and abusively when we sense that the other person wants or needs to be criticized, or to be degraded. The shark-teeth of abuse bare themselves and, if our partner endures the humiliation for anything more than a second, we zero in until we draw emotional blood. These kinds of relationships are, of course, common. Early mild criticism leads to later major criticism; early demands lead to later major demands; early rage has the potential for tissue damage in the later stages.

3. The critical voice also appears when our potential mate reminds us of a particular time, person, or event in our life. For example, if we had an abusive relationship with our parents when we were younger, we might experience "post traumatic stress," a disorder often characterized by the need to "act out" certain feelings and behaviors that we were forced to swallow when we were too helpless to resist. This phenomenon commonly occurs during wartime when soldiers and noncombatants experience the trauma of battle and the accompanying violence.

If someone abused us as children, we will often become abusive as adults. If we have been beaten or frightened as children, or if we have witnessed violence in one form or another, the chances are that we will become an adult at risk for violence. The wrath of the unconscious but fully activated critical (violent) voice we ingested as youngsters is the reaction to seemingly innocent comments by our lover.

Often our desire to protect ourselves—and our desire to avoid dealing with our own discomfort—is converted to a desire to protect and to defend those who also have flaws, or who also are confused and frightened. As a result, we may begin to campaign for assistance for the homeless, become volunteers at the local hospital, or become consumed by the plights of unborn children.

The path of our passions, of course, is dictated by the "voices." If the uncritical parent voice dominates, we are prone to invest our energies in a venture of altruism. The altruism may simply take the form of contributions to a charity or volunteerism. In the extreme, however, it may take the form of self-sacrifice (and perhaps self-destruction) to protect the less fortunate.

If the never-satisfied, demanding, finger-pointing voice of the critical parent dominates, we most likely involve ourselves in pursuits that are dictatorial in nature. At one end of the "dictatorial" spectrum, we find the harsh but well-

34   Couples at the Crossroad

meaning parent who simply wants to raise his child properly; at the other end, we find the mean-spirited bully who subjugates entire nations.

The passion displayed by Mike and Ann is the same kind of passion most of us know quite well. Often the voices say the same kind of things: "Do this" or "Do not do that," or "Let me out of here"! How we negotiate the demands of the voices, however, differs from person to person.

We may make excuses for our behavior and withdraw from the scene. We may recall personal experiences, or the vignettes played out between our parents, and create a voice (uncritical parent) which assures us that all will be OK. Or perhaps we reframe the scene, and pull the fangs out of the fearful/hurtful situation, making it less toxic by giving it "more perspective."

If we are truly creative, we figure out a way not only to overcome the obstacle to our happiness, but also to maintain a sense of pride and dignity.

During the beginning phases of our love relationships, the passion we feel is a romantic passion of excitement, giddiness, playfulness, mild insecurity, and a strong desire for physical closeness. As the relationship evolves and matures, other passions subsume these feelings. We develop a passion for protectiveness, a passion for acceptance, and a passion for establishing a partnership.

In order to help Ann and Mike better understand the impact of the "voices" of passion I asked them to complete the following exercise:

Remember your (1) first contact, (2) first real date, (3) first time you became intimate (either sexually or emotionally or both). Recall the "voices" you heard from each other. Were they whiny, playful, disappointed, intimidating, pouty, stubborn, sexy, demanding, sweet, and frightened?

Ann was the first one to speak. She related her feelings on their first date. "Mike called to ask me out to dinner. It was the first time we had really considered the possibility of dating although we each knew we were attracted to the other. I remember his voice during the telephone call. It was so uncertain, so insecure, that I remember thinking that I wished I could make this easier for him. Even then, I wanted to protect him and make him feel ok about the whole situation. The voice I heard was the frightened voice—at least initially—but then, after I said I would love to go out for dinner with him, the voice changed, and he became sort of playful, and we both became giggly. I remember feeling like I did when I was in high school and I had a crush on one of the football players, only this time it was a softer, gentler feeling. Not that I didn't feel sexy, but I also felt something deeper. Then one time when I told Mike that my son Jason was ill, he became so attentive—not in a sticky sort of way—just attentive. The voice I heard let me know everything was going to be all right and that I could always

Voices　35

count on him. I do not know about the other voices you mentioned. Of course, we have always had passionate discussions about writing and about politics, friendly debates with lots of sparks flying. They're always fun. Other than that, I don't remember any other voices. Wait, maybe when he's really working hard on a project, I hear the voice that seems to need a lot of approval. It's as though he's asking someone to really care about him and what he does. I often wonder what happens if the voice inside his head rejects him and his projects. Maybe that's why he works so hard all the time."

Mike began to tell us about his "voices."

"I remember that first talk we had on the phone. You're right. I was scared. I wanted you to say exactly what you finally did say—that you would be delighted to have dinner with me. I did not realize my voice came across like a frightened child's voice. But you're right about that part. The funny thing is that even though I do not remember precisely how I felt, I do remember your voice. You were so gentle, so kind, that whatever fear I had just seemed to melt away. I knew at that point that you were somebody very special. Nobody had ever been able to make me feel that way. When we went to the restaurant—I think it was in Copley Place—everything was like an adventure. The food we ordered, the bottle of wine, the way you looked at me. The only voice I heard was a romantic and gentle voice. I wanted to skip down the street with you and just hold your hand and touch you. Your voices comforted me and made me feel that somehow I fit into your life. It was a strange feeling for me, because I'd been raised to be self-sufficient and I do not let people in too often. You mentioned Jason's illness. What you sensed in me was accurate. I wanted to let you know that I would stand by your side and Jason's side too for as long as it took him to get better. I did not realize my feelings came through, but I'm glad you got the message. You are right about another one of my voices. I've never thought about it before, but when I get into one of my projects, I hear two voices. One tells me that I'm really pretty bright and I'm going to win the lawsuit—or whatever the project happens to be. But sometimes I hear a voice telling me that I'm not working hard enough, that I do not deserve to win the case, and no matter how hard I'm willing to work, I'm not acceptable. I do not know whose voice I hear. I think it's a male voice—maybe not—I can't say for sure. I usually end up feeling tired and I want to sleep or sometimes, when the voice is too strong, I just want to drink myself into a stupor. Since I've met you, I don't hear that voice too often."

"Thank goodness," Ann laughed.

Ann and Mike picked up a variety of messages from each other—largely at an unconscious level. The messages had been distilled from the words, the inflection, the intensity, and the benevolence of the voices that each one had introjected—swallowed—as a child. Some of the voices were digested and became part of the person's personality. Some of the voices, however, could never be fully digested because they were alien to his self-image.

The "frightened voice" that Mike experienced was uncomfortable for him because it simply did not fit into the image of himself that he had developed over the years. Likewise, the "needy" voice he experienced was the antithesis of the self-sufficient individual he was raised to believe he was. Yet these voices influenced every behavior and every decision that Mike made. Ann was able to subdue the power of the needy feelings by giving Mike unspoken permission to feel helpless and needy. She also responded to his sexiness and his playfulness, feelings that were encouraged by neither Mike's intellectualized father nor his business-like ex-wife.

Ann's voices also influenced her decision-making. Her Playful Child enjoyed Mike taking her out for dinner. Ann could be sexy and playful. At the same time, given Mike's nervousness about possible rejection, she could help alleviate his apprehension by using a protective and gentle voice she learned from her mother and reinforced by her father. She said she really loved the opportunity to nurture him, maybe even mother him a little, while at the same time she could feel the excitement of the physical and emotional closeness that she felt.

Passion is an essential ingredient in most relationships. However, passion is not simply the desire to be romantic; it is a desire to strike a harmonic balance. It is a path formed by many influences. It is a biological life force expressing itself through a thousand voices we have swallowed—voices we now use to attract our potential mate and to repel our potential enemies. The trick is to match the correct voice—the correct passion—with the correct recipient in a balanced fashion. Too much of the uncritical parent leads to an unrealistic degree of playfulness; too much of the critical parent leads to rage and/or withdrawal. How much is too much is a decision each person must make in her own way. However, we must make a decision; a relationship without balanced passions is simply one of life's good meals without the spices to make it a great one.

4

Toxic Personalities

Several personal life styles can become "toxic" to any love relationship. Fortunately, we can usually spot potential problems after the first few dates—if we trust our senses. Some of the people with "toxic" personalities are simply odd, annoying, or unappealing; others, however, can be extremely harmful and we should avoid them. In all cases, they can become "crazy makers."

Listening to my descriptions of toxic personalities, Ann noted with a smile, "But we're all like that!" Indeed we are, but *most* of us—at least *most* of the time—do not make other people feel crazy.

Crazy makers are people who make us feel edgy and frustrated. The first four crazy makers have personality styles that most of us find difficult to deal with. Since they are core personality types whose behaviors and symptoms form the bases of many of the others, we want to describe them in detail. While reading the following material and the vignettes that accompany them, think about your lover or, if presently not dating, to your last lover, and become aware of similarities between them and the characters described. (If you have the courage, you might also note whether any of *your* behavior is toxic to somebody else.)

The Obsessive Thinker

The Obsessive Thinker is robotic, highly efficient, regimented, detail-oriented, deliberate, and persistent. Unfortunately, he is also rigid in his thinking, driven in his behavior, and confused about what is socially acceptable.

He sets himself apart from others because of his strong opinions, and his narrow definitions about what is right and what is wrong. There are no gray areas in his life. He is oppositional and negative—at least superficially. When we listen closely, however, we find something even more annoying. We find that we become frustrated, not because of any real negative contact, but because there is no real contact at all. We get the feeling we are talking into a cobweb.

Except for an occasional attentive gaze, there is no indication that he hears our words, or that he has understood our message. If we offer an observation or an opinion, the Obsessive Thinker generally responds with a "yes...but." The maddening part of the exchange is the never-satisfied tone of his responses; it is as though he asks us for our thoughts, but will not acknowledge them once they are given.

At a deeper level, the Obsessive Thinker's problem is his inability to pay attention. He misses the whole point of the conversation. He simply cannot shift gears and come up with a different way of looking at things. He is distracted by a particular point of view and rigidly adheres to it—not necessarily in a nasty or hostile manner, although his irritability is clear.

The whole of his existence, intellectual and emotional, lies in the details of any given situation. He exudes intensity—a narrowing of focus—that excludes the larger picture of life. Casualness and spontaneity are subjugated to a microscopic regard for non-essentials. The tiniest scratch on a recording becomes more important than the melody of the song.

The Obsessive Thinker generally is productive. In fact, he produces all the time. Long hours, hard work, and intense concern about his level of achievement impress supervisor and workmates alike. Nonetheless, rather than stir up feelings of admiration, his successes are regarded as an oddity or, even worse, not regarded at all. His attention to detail consumes him. He sees his goals clearly and strives toward perfection. As a worker, he involves himself in minutiae, often choosing jobs that require technical skill rather than "people skills."

What makes him so unique is the almost constant need to put forth effort, a need that taxes the patience of co-workers and lovers alike. The Obsessive Thinker is always trying—trying to succeed, trying to do better, and trying to maintain a semblance of order in his life through activity. That his inner voices exclude playfulness is a trait that makes him a poor candidate for the casual date.

If you listen to the Obsessive Thinker for even a few minutes, you will hear many references to what people "should" or "ought to" do. His speech is riddled with finger pointing words—words that bring guilt and shame. But, again, he doesn't really mean it; he just can't help it. The pressure he exerts on others, and the anxieties he experiences ad nauseum are the result of the many "shoulds" he swallowed early in life. His wishes, whimsical thoughts, spontaneity, and anything else that distracts him from putting order in his life produces restlessness and tension.

Under the pressure of this anxiety, the tiny cracks in his personality widen, and, instead of a highly efficient and productive man, we see a taskmaster grappling with the possibility of losing control.

A key concept here is "role." For the Obsessive Thinker, a "role" is the schematic of the *shoulds* and *have to's* of his life.

The role serves as a skeletal outline he fills in with appropriate expectations and procedures. He says to himself, "I am (my role is) a lover, therefore I should do such and such..." or "I am an engineer, therefore I have to do such and such..." He colors in the *shoulds* of his life with what he regards as acceptable behavior. Any deviation is punished by the all-pervasive worry that he is doing something wrong. We realize before the end of the first date that the Obsessive Thinker's religion is orderliness, and that his rigidity will more than likely prevent us from full involvement in his life.

Ironically, the Obsessive Thinker's steadfast reliance on making correct decisions about what is acceptable belies his near helplessness in decision-making. Because he is so concerned with the rightness of his decisions, he tries to balance the pluses and the minuses of any decision—over and over, and over again. He constantly worries and struggles. He constantly weighs consequences (butchers and Obsessive Thinkers weigh everything!). He becomes obsessed with right answers and proper behavior until he is exhausted—and until he exhausts us.

Imagine the agony of the Obsessive Thinker when asked what color suit he likes or what kind of wallpaper he would like in his living room. The problem again is the absence of a rule—the absence of a *should* that automatically dictates a right answer.

The Obsessive Thinker has another trait that sets him apart. His unrealistic thoughts often go hand in hand with compulsive behaviors. For example, handwashing rituals, counting numbers, and picking lint off clothing serve as anxiety relievers; and, in severe cases, these rituals become magical contrivances to guard against powerlessness and bad luck. This indeed makes him a very difficult person to live with—and to love.

The Suspicious Thinker

Suspicious Thinkers also pay attention to details. However, they are interested in a different kind of detail. Obsessive thinkers pay attention to minutiae—the details of details. The Suspicious Thinker, on the other hand, is focused on subtle behaviors—glances, words, suggestions, and facial expressions—that he suspects are designed to trick him. He becomes apprehensive, anxious, and preoccupied

40 Couples at the Crossroad

with the thought that someone is out to get him. No amount of talking, arguing, or logic can convince him otherwise.

When the Suspicious Thinker's distrust is chronic, the resulting emotional climate is tense and extremely uncomfortable. The level of discomfort affects all three dimensions of love: passion, intimacy, and commitment. His relationships suffer because of his keen perception and his often brilliant insight, as much as from his suspicious scrutiny. In short, he won't let people get away with a thing. He seems to see everything and to know everything. At least he sees whatever he needs to see in order to confirm his suspicions.

He tells us he wants to get to the "bottom line," the "essence" of the relationship. He says he wants to deflate pretense and sham, and to enter into an "honest" relationship. However, what he really wants is a careful analysis of events, from which is excluded any information that contradicts his suspicions.

He scrutinizes pictures, documents, agreements, and math problems with gusto. He is hyperalert and sensitive to anything out of the ordinary. He tells us he is searching for truth, but we wonder whether his real motivation is to find the truth before the truth finds him. The climate of his relationships reflects confusion and unpredictability—emotions that do not enhance fun, humor, a casual date, a good-morning breakfast, or an honest disagreement.

In part, the Suspicious Thinker is motivated by the need to know precisely what is going on in the relationship. When we look carefully at his actions, however, we see that he is interested in something more, namely, in discovering his "truth" at the cost of our credibility. His self-righteousness, his finger-pointer attitudes, his intrusiveness, and his insistence on "honesty" dampen a night on the town. He resists our attempts to confront him with logic; temper outbursts, and, of course, suspiciousness follows any attempt on our part to inject reason into a debate of issues.

Everyday experiences that most of us take for granted become "clues" to the Suspicious Thinker. What he sees is exactly what we see, but he interprets its significance differently. He draws connections between experiences that most of us would not.

Most of us would agree, for example, that taxes are necessary; the Suspicious Thinker, however, carries the idea further. He may believe it is part of a government plot to rob us of our money, to subjugate us, and to "keep the little guy in his place." Though we generally see socialism as an economic and social philosophy, the Suspicious Thinker might see it as part of a global political takeover. (Of course, the suspicious Socialist sees Capitalism in the same light.) While the Obsessive Thinker sees the details of details and yearns for perfectionism, the

Suspicious Thinker searches for imperfections that become the clues to imagined schemes and manipulations.

Suspicious Thinkers involved in a relationship become possessive and jealous. A lover observed to receive an innocent kiss from a family friend becomes a partner in an affair. The boss who shows up late for an appointment becomes part of the plot to force the Suspicious Thinker's resignation. The slightest rejection—a grimace or smile at the wrong time, a subtle attempt at correction—meets with a look of tension, close investigation, and perhaps even rage.

Most of us are able to shrug off rejection. We use our social skills to push them aside, or we simply repress the incident and get on with our lives. Often, we are able to use humor to defuse our annoyance, or to mollify our anxious concerns. Not so, with the Suspicious Thinker who is more likely to become enraged and vindictive. At this point in a relationship, the tension becomes so draining and so uncomfortable that the habitually Suspicious Thinker becomes a person we most want to avoid. Fortunately, while all Suspicious Thinkers distort reality to some degree, and while most can drive us crazy with their suspicions and jealousy, most do respond to love and caring.

The Non-Thinker

The Non Thinker does not see the details of the details, nor does he search for clues of a "plot" or "trickery." He sees the world as a bunch of unconnected dots onto which he projects his fears and wishes. He is an impressionist. He is not interested in facts or objective data. Introduced to a stranger, he may gush, "S/he's great," "Wonderful," or "Unbelievable," or perhaps, "S/he's awful," "Disgusting," or "Nerdy," without any information whatsoever upon which to base his conclusions.

The Non Thinker senses the world. Colors are readily transmuted to shapes and sounds. The sight of a full moon or the music of Vivaldi readily induces an altered state of consciousness; the bizarre juxtapositions of a Picasso painting induce feelings of sadness or anger as much as they inspire awe. Paris is not simply Paris: It is a bouquet of flowers in a field of weeds. Asked to explain his perceptions, he responds, "It just looks that way—I do not know why."

Unlike the Obsessive Thinker or the Suspicious Thinker, the Non Thinker depends on immediate sensations and hunches. He lacks the persistence and narrowed focus we see in the other kinds of crazy makers. He is neither overdriven, nor terribly efficient, nor intellectually curious, although he is often capable of creative problem solving. He becomes easily distracted, goes off on tangents, and

42   Couples at the Crossroad

his thinking is hard to follow. Unusual ideas grab his attention; he is susceptible to compelling outside influences. We get the impression that he is dragged from pillar to post by anything he finds stimulating—emotions, words, colors, or sounds.

Emotionally, he is given to quick changes. He can be easily embarrassed, overwhelmed with grief, full of apologies, become silly and giddy, and exhibit tantrums—all within a brief few moments. He flits from one stimulus to another and from one subject to another without the benefit of control or good judgment. Bad feelings and good feelings become fused into one global undifferentiated response to his immediate surroundings.

The unique characteristic of the Non Thinker is his shallow existence. Emotions flow abundantly, but we're left with the impression that the Non Thinker doesn't really feel them at all. He reminds us of a character in a cartoon.

His emotions are interchangeable. The quantity of any particular emotion appears to be just as important as the quality of it. He lives on the theatrical stage, giving the impression that his entire life is a facade. His *as if* existence is annoying, because we simply cannot touch the *real* him—the part of him that is most important.

Rather than meaningful responses, the Non Thinker gives knee jerk reactions that are superficial and frustrating. If confronted with genuine feelings, he shows surprise; he simply doesn't know he is an actor in a play he has written years ago. Ironically, the Non Thinker is as ignorant about his feelings as the Obsessive Thinker is about his feelings. Asked how he feels, he might very well say, "I really do not know…" He might even be aware enough to tell us that his feelings are alien to him—that they come from somewhere outside him and do not really belong to him at all. This makes it all the more difficult for his lover; if he doesn't own his feelings, then he certainly can't know what he genuinely feels about the people around him.

Not only does the Non Thinker not understand his own emotions, he doesn't understand other people's emotions either. He may act *as if* he is angry or annoyed, but then becomes thoroughly confused when others respond to him in a like manner. He fails to notice that, although he experiences his behavior as play-acting, most other people really mean it when they become angry (sad, caring, etc.). His naïveté in these matters is almost unbelievable. Color his emotional climate "cold."

The Impulsive Thinker

Impulsive Thinkers and Non Thinkers have something in common: They are both overwhelmed by their impulses. The Non Thinker is stimulated by vivid, forceful impressions of a poorly organized world. The Impulsive Thinker is driven by whimsy, and by the feeling, "I just feel like doing it." Both types of Thinkers are passive recipients of a world filled with temptation—a world that seems to beckon them to react immediately with little regard to consequence.

The Impulsive Thinker is in fact a Non Thinker who does not even enjoy the guidance of an *as if* existence. He does not act as *if* he is following a script, nor does he act as *if* he is pretending. His impulses are pure. Life is simple: He wants it, so he takes it. There is no intention or planning; there are few controls—either internal or external. There is just stimulation. His reactions are quick, abrupt, and ill conceived. If we listen carefully, we hear the Impulsive Thinker saying things like, "I do not know why I did it—I just did," or "I did not mean to do it—it just happened," or perhaps "I did not mean to do it—I just couldn't help myself."

Whimsy and overwhelming urges characterize The Impulsive Thinker's nature. In his world, urges supplant reason and logic; stimulation replaces deliberateness and planning. We find these characteristics, in varying degrees, among many alcoholics, drug addicts, narcissists, and psychopathic personalities.

To a lesser degree, they appear in the behavior of most people who enjoy spontaneity. When coupled with internal controls (a conscience), whimsy, and spontaneity lead to a joyous experience of life; without internal controls, they most often lead to unhappiness—especially for others.

Impulsive Thinkers give in to external pressure—whim, urge, or temptation. Something "out there" pulls them and "makes" them do things they know are not quite normal, but they do it anyway. The idea of will power or deliberation is foreign to them. That they themselves are responsible for their actions is likewise a foreign idea to them.

All of us experience temptation. What makes the Impulsive Thinker different is the degree and the percentage of time he is "tempted." We all are tempted to buy something we do not particularly need, but most of us won't grab a handbag or break the window of a jewelry store because we "just couldn't help it." Most of us will not go against the grain of social acceptability if it means ostracism. Most of us will not do it on a regular basis.

What sets the Impulsive Thinker apart from most people is his quick, unpredictable, and potentially dangerous behavior. Most of us enjoy whimsy within the context of a stable life style where one event follows another in a natural manner. The Impulsive Thinker's behavior however is generally erratic and poorly planned.

His assessment of social rules and regulations is simply different and alien to most of us. For example, while most of us are willing to postpone immediate gratification ("I want what I want, but I'll wait a bit."), the Impulsive Thinker has little appreciation of the notion called "patience" or "delay." He takes what is available, when it is available: an unattended wallet, a "scam" promising much but delivering little. In short, he buys into any situation offering stimulation. His motto seems to be "Damn the torpedoes, full speed ahead," even when the course is fraught with danger for him or for others.

What seems to be lacking is a concept of "worry." Unlike the Obsessive Thinker who worries constantly—who weighs and tries to balance all decisions—the Impulsive Thinker seldom shows concern about his choices.

He seems to lack the voice of an effective critical parent who teaches a deep sense of morality and ethics. The result, in its most obvious form, is the relative ease with which the Impulsive Thinker lies, manipulates, and exhibits marked degrees of insincerity. These traits are crazy-makers, and they are the very same traits that prevent long term planning—planning that in many cases includes us.

The Obsessive Thinker, the Suspicious Thinker, the Non Thinker, and the Impulsive Thinker represent personality styles that drive us to distraction. The Obsessive Thinker is always worrying and weighing consequences. By the time, he gets through assessing the details of details, searching for perfection, producing piles of paper at work, and ritualizing his behavior, we're ready to throw in the towel. After all, how much can we take? However, Obsessive Thinkers are not always unlovable. They often make for very tidy, well-meaning mates for people who can overlook their eccentricities.

The Suspicious Thinker is a bit more difficult to love. His groundless suspicions, his continuous search for trickery, his jealousy, and his possessiveness give us the feeling of being owned rather than being loved. But, then again, some people like that feeling! If his overly suspicious view of the world is not too severe, he can convince us his perceptions are accurate, and a tenuous but tempestuous relationship is a possibility.

The Non Thinker often can be quite appealing because of his impressionistic view of the world, his creative attempts at making sense out of it, and his tendency to be highly theatrical. We tend to overlook his forgetfulness and lack of functional intelligence because of his charm, superficial sexiness, and the promise of excitement in the future. As the relationship matures, however, the absence of real intimacy becomes more apparent; and this lack of intimacy eats away at the relationship like termites on a succulent wood-frame house. The result, after a period, is a feeling of exhaustion and loneliness. Nonetheless, we often regard the Non Thinker as a sweet, naïve, zestful lover who commands our attention.

The Impulsive Thinker can also be loveable. He is unpredictable, exciting, whimsical, capricious, and—when he chooses to be—very attentive. If his impulsivity is not too severe, he conjures up a sense of adventure and mystery. Women addicted to "love" often find themselves involved with this kind of person, despite the absolute predictability of trouble in the future.

Ann and Mike seemed to have a good time discussing these personality styles. Mike pointed out how his father had many of the characteristics of the Obsessive Thinker. His preoccupation with details, his moral judgments about the rectitude of certain religious, his philosophical convictions, and his indecisiveness despite strong opinions were all qualities that Mike could identify. Of course, Ann reminded him that he, Mike, often displayed the same behaviors. Fortunately, for both of them, Mike had a sense of humor and strong affection for Ann, who could melt his obsessive thoughts with a touch and a smile.

Ann also recognized her own tendency to behave in a non-thinker fashion. She liked to connect the dots between real experiences and her fantasies; that, after all, was what her writing was all about. She liked the combination of strong impressions, the freedom to *ooh* and *ahh* at life's never-ending kaleidoscope of happenings, and her skill as a teller of stories. Mike said what he liked even more was her ability to balance her wonderful spontaneity with common sense. Here was one instance where the Obsessive Thinker and the Non-Thinker complemented each other's life style. The result was a sense of contentment and personal satisfaction. But, Mike wondered, if that was so, why wasn't he 100 percent sure that the relationship would work out? (Ann did not remind him that Obsessive Thinkers always wonder that!)

The four basic personality types often create an emotional climate that is so hostile or cold, that the only way to prevent emotional hypothermia is to withdraw from the relationship. However, they are by no means the only crazy-makers we encounter in our search for a soul mate. Here are several others you will recognize immediately:

"The Trapper"

Known for his skill as a manipulator, The "Trapper" seduces us with his "helplessness," inviting us in to "save" him. Once we take the bait, he changes his helpless role. He becomes the aggressor, and we end up feeling embarrassed and foolish. More importantly, we end up wondering about our sanity.

Here is a typical scenario: One partner tells the other he is tired of making all the decisions, and then he demands that she assume more responsibility. She does her best to relieve him of the burden. The first partner rejects not only the results of her efforts, but the effort itself. (Of course, they play the same scene repeatedly for years on end). The resultant anger, frustration, and feeling of betrayal are enough to make us swear off dating for months. "Trappers" are magnificently effective crazy-makers!

"The Double Binder"

Many mental health specialists have implicated the "Double Binder" as a primary cause of emotional illness. The essential ingredient of the double bind is the "mixed message." The "Double Binder" sends two communications, each one exclusive of the other. The husband says to his wife, for example, "The kids and I need you at home," and then goes on to suggest, "We need more money...you'll need to find a second job." Examples of this kind of crazy-making are numerous.

Here is another instance: Mother tells her teenage daughter to eat everything on her plate, then comments negatively on the daughter's weight gain. Common responses to the double message are withdrawal, frustration, and regression. As the child becomes older, aggressive behavior may increase. The same responses occur in love relationships, and the emotional climate becomes toxic. We should studiously avoid The "Double Binder" : His level toxicity is extremely virulent.

The "Intimacy from Ten Feet Away" (IFTFA) Person

This crazy-maker pulls his lover in, while at the same time he pushes her away. Like the "Double Binder," the IFTFA Person sends two messages, both equally strong. One message—often the verbal one—implies that the crazy-maker finds his lover attractive and wants her to share his physical and emotional boundaries.

His lover, however, experiences something different: She experiences a rejection. The closer she tries to get, the harsher the rejection becomes. It is as though IFTFA Person wants to experience all the benefits of a love relationship without having to tolerate the presence of another human. The "Push-Pull" reflects a problem at the contact boundary. In its most severe form, the phenomenon takes on psychotic proportions. Fears of Abandonment and fears of Intrusion on the part of the crazy-maker produce marked distortions of reality. Interestingly, despite the fact that the situation often is impossible to resolve, breaking away from IFTFA is extremely difficult because we often believe the IFTFA PERSON when he tries to convince us that the next time he really will mean it when he says, "I love you."

"The Whiner"

Male or female, the Whiner has the dubious distinction of being utterly objectionable within the first twenty minutes of meeting. His/her whining begins with a fingernails-on-the-chalk-board bleating about an octave higher than our comfort zone. S/he goes on and on...and on. The vocal qualities of the Whiner are simply dreadful.

More repulsive, however, is his/her negativism, which reverberates through every word. The negativism has the power to bring us down, to dilute whatever happiness and joy we might be feeling at the time. It reminds us of a 3 AM feeding with a colicky infant who won't be satisfied no matter how much we coo and rock.

The emotional climate created is a constant chill with no signs of a warming sun. We need only to count the number of hairs raised on the backs of our necks to discover how much we want to avoid a repeated encounter with the Whiner.

"The Armadillo"

The Armadillo buries himself with a seductive silence that leads us to presume competence. He doesn't let anyone in. He is armored, withholding, and tough. His boundaries are sacrosanct: There is a brightly lit sign over his head that says, "Do not tread on me." He presents himself as the strong silent type but, in truth, he is simply guarded and unwilling to share. We often regard him as "mysterious"—a trait that is dangerously appealing to many women.

It does not take long for us to realize that his strength is a sham. Once we get beyond the first layer of his personality, we learn there is no substance. However, always there is a lingering doubt; we wonder what surprises he might have in store—if we only could break through the tough exterior. He is a crazy-maker because like the IFTFA he keeps us coming back even when we fully realize that the relationship will go nowhere. As far as the emotional climate goes—brrrr!

48   Couples at the Crossroad

"The Possessor"

The Possessor is closely related to the Obsessive Thinker, on the one hand, and to the Suspicious Thinker, on the other. Feelings of closeness and devotion become fused with feelings of possessiveness and jealousy. He swings from despair to excitement and back again before we realize what is happening. He searches everywhere for assurance that his lover won't abandon him, that she loves him, and won't betray him.

He needs to know that he is more important than the business meeting, a night out with the girls, or a visit to family in another state. He reminds us of a three-year-old who clings onto Mommy as she heads off to work. He also does something even more objectionable: He marks us with his scent so that others will know who the real owner is. The "scent" of course may take different forms: a costly gift, a special hairstyle, a tattoo, or even pieces of clothing deliberately left at our apartment to remind us that we belong only to him. By the time, we figure out what is really happening, it is almost too late, we have already been "owned."

Despite this, the Possessor is extremely powerful. He is often exciting (when not depressed or angry) and attentive. If we can withstand the feeling of being trapped and we are as needy as the Possessor is, a symbiotic albeit caring relationship is possible. However, for most of us, The Possessor is a crazy-maker that induces resentment, fear, and emotional withdrawal. The resulting emotional climate reminds us of a line in the old folk song, "Oh, Suzannah" ("…the sun's so hot I froze to death…").

Stage II
Connection

5

Connecting

If we survive confrontation and/or sexual contact with our lover, we might be lucky enough to enter Stage II, falling in love. Our perceptions become distorted to varying degrees; our judgment is often based on our wishes and fears rather than on the dictates of reality. The true nature of the relationship is not yet clear. Nonetheless, we feel connected.

During the first stage of coupling, we are first concerned with attracting someone we *think* we want to be with, and secondly we attempt to separate the wheat from the chaff. If our eyes are working properly and we have our wits about us, the task is relatively easy. We consider the overall quality of the contact: the motives, the level of toxicity, the emotional climate for coupling, and the way the potential mate was raised (including his burdens, his trainers, and his ownership). We also study his voices: if they are too strident, too sappy, too frightened, too angry, and too happy, it will be obvious to us.

What most of us are looking for is a guy or gal who is responsive, nurturing, and playful; one who doesn't make us feel crazy or compromised by his destructive behaviors and his incessant demands for attention and time; one whose motivation and emotional climate are compatible with our own motivation for coupling and our own emotional comfort zone. In short, most of us are looking for someone we want to go to bed with at night and want to wake up with in the morning.

Now we are at a different level in the relationship. We have already eliminated individuals who do not fit the bill; instead, we have connected with our tentative mate of choice and we are now committed—but not completely. Before committing ourselves completely, we need to look at a few more things.

We are at a different crossroad now and we need to make different decisions. How do we know we're in love? Shall we commit ourselves or not? Do we really feel "intimate" with each other or was the closeness we felt before just a passing

52   Couples at the Crossroad

mood phase? Can we really tolerate each other's life styles? Or rather, shall we find ourselves feeling trapped and unhappy in years to come?

Whereas the decisions at Stage I can be relatively easy to make, the decisions we need to make during Stage II involve intimacy, moods, and life scripts. None of the factors are easy to understand and none of the decisions are simple, but decisions have to be made nonetheless.

The Seven Signs of Love

How do we know when we are in Stage II in the first place? How do we know when we are really falling in love? Ann asked this question during one of our early sessions.

How do we know we are in love? Here are a few of the signs:

1. *We want exclusive companionship* with our partner. We experience a sense of loss and a sense of emptiness when we are apart. At night, we yearn to retreat into our lover's arms. We take on our lover's perception of reality. Our boundaries become fused (and often con-fused). Our souls and minds join until we feel part of, yet separate from, each other.

2. *We want to share* our feelings, our thoughts, our experiences, and ourselves. We discover that too much talk can disrupt the easy flow of feelings between two people in the successful coupling mode. We learn that a gentle look, a kindness, an unexpected gift, a card on an unbirthday—all these often mean much more than talk.

3. We discover that we must balance the acts of giving and taking. *We learn how to give and take* according to our need, our energy, our generosity, and our assertiveness. Most of us—if we are truly in love—learn how and when to give affection freely and how and when to accept it freely. A mature relationship cannot survive without this sense of balance.

4. With the increase in our intimacy and commitment, *we develop more trust*. During the "falling in love" stage, we test the waters and learn what our lover and we can expect from the relationship. If the evolutionary forces are working properly, we weed out our "bad" matches and those that remain will, at least in theory, lead to mutual trust, a sense of loyalty, and faith that all problems will eventually work themselves out. At this point, we are willing to open ourselves up, willing to make ourselves vulnerable and sensitive to rejection. We develop

the unshakable notion that our lover would never deliberately do anything to harm us.

5. *We learn to establish a balance between possessiveness and tolerance.* Possessiveness is born of the universal need to enjoy the exclusive rights to our lover's mind and body. Tolerance involves an acceptance of him as a being separate from us, a being with a life of his own. However, along with our feelings of passion and intimacy comes the feeling of ownership, a feeling that he will be there for us as long as we want him to be.

This possessive attitude is not entirely without benefit: When we apply it realistically, our lover will enjoy the exclusivity of the relationship, because, after all, exclusivity is the very essence of couplehood.

The adult part of us does not always enjoy the idea of "owning" someone, an idea that seems to sneak into the bedroom like an unwanted guest. However, the child in us—the part of us that is insecure and uncertain—wants our partner to spend his energy and his time with us. His time is our time; his energy is our energy.

Work, hobbies, pastimes, friends, relatives, and sometimes—perhaps more often than we would like to admit—even the children become rivals for the attention we have come to believe properly belongs to us. When the time, the energy, and the affection are not forthcoming, we often become mildly resentful, mildly jealous, mildly suspicious, and mildly sad.

Balancing the need to "own" our lover and the equally strong need to tolerate separation from him influences the quality of our love in a powerful manner. If the balancing act fails, we begin to vacillate between holding on too tight and letting go too much, overshooting the mark, retracting blurted out comments, recanting legitimately held positions, always trying to re-synchronize the emotional seesaw.

The man is in the "Hold Me Tight" emotional state while making love, and the "Let Me Loose" emotional state shortly thereafter, often feeling guilty that he has given too much of his passion and not enough of his compassion during the act. The woman means "Hold Me Tight" while making love and "Keep Holding Me Tight" until I have to fix my hair in the morning, then "Let Me Loose" (that is, no hanky-panky until I feel pretty again). The man wants his lover to "Hold Me Tight" (rub my back, fix me a drink, tell me how smart I am, etc.) when he has had a tough day at work but wants her to "Let Me Loose" to go bowling with his buddies. The woman, on the other hand, wants her lover to "Hold Me Tight" (hold my hand, tell me you love me, tell me how pretty I am, etc.) on the dance floor, but wants him "Let Me Loose" (give me time alone with my friends, do not call me too much at work, etc.) when she wants to maintain a sense of independence and self-sufficiency.

The exchanges may be harsh or gentle, spirited or subdued, but always they are designed to establish a harmonious beat to our dancing souls. If we are healthy and we have developed a sense of optimism, we will reach equilibrium. We will begin to recognize when to hold on and when to let loose. Shared moments will be nurturing and uplifting.

If, on the other hand, after much effort, we cannot balance the emotional seesaw, something is very much wrong with the connection, and the coupling process will not proceed.

6. *We are willing to ensure our lover's safety and comfort to a greater degree than our own.* The emotional climate of our relationship is one of total spiritual giving, of transcending our own financial, physical, and emotional welfare for the sake of our partner's. The fact that our partner, if the partnership is an equal one, also develops a self-sacrificing attitude prevents a lopsided altruism, an unhealthy one-way relationship that leads to feelings of resentment or, in more serious cases, masochistic self-sacrifice.

7. *We discover that sex is only one dimension of a three-dimensional love.* As such, a fully matured love—with certain exceptions—cannot blossom until there is a union of bodies and souls. The self-sacrificing quality of a loving relationship, except in cases where one of the partners has a severe disability, requires that we offer our sexual selves completely and that our partner reciprocate. A great part of this is simple biology; a greater part is the desire to please, to be pleased, and then to merge as one being. A majority of couples need regular, consistent, and tender sexual attention in order to make the relationship complete.

Abstinence for extended periods, that is, until we begin to feel deprived, is a sign of serious difficulties with the coupling process, protestations notwithstanding. On the other hand, there are relationships that have none of the qualities of love except for high sexual activity. Such a one-dimensional love is two dimensions short of completion. A passion/sex-only relationship will leave us battling low self-esteem as we advance in age and intimacy and commitment become more important to us. Ninety percent of the time, enjoyable, spontaneous, and tender sex on a regular basis combined with feelings of intimacy and commitment is the litmus test of a relationship. At any given time, we need only to assess the quality of our loving to determine quality of our love.

Were Mike and Ann in love? Mike and Ann had experienced many of the "signs" of love within three months of their first meeting. During Stage I, their contact was sharp. Mike reported that when he and Ann first met, a thunderbolt coursed through his spine. After they explored common interests, they continued to be attracted to each other, and courtship and physical contact followed.

Along with the more subtle adjustment to each other's needs and desires, they had matched and sorted experiences in an attempt to make the major pieces of life—religion, desire for children, politics, values—fit together without too much strain. Enough pieces came together, and they discovered enough passion to glue the pieces in place. Moreover, all the signs were there: They both wanted an exclusive relationship along with shared thoughts, feelings, and experiences. They were protective of each other and enjoyed giving and taking from each other. And the sex! They agreed they had never felt as sexy as they did when they were with each other.

Clearly, Ann and Mike had discovered strange and wonderful although not always comfortable feelings developing inside them. They had discovered the need for physical and emotional closeness, the need to share, the tendency to feel jealous, and the desire to sacrifice their happiness to ensure the other's happiness.

In response to Ann's question about love, I answered:

"How do you know whether you're in love? It is pretty simple: Add the desire to go to bed together at night with the desire to wake up and face the world together in the morning. The sum should leave you feeling happy, fulfilled, and mildly euphoric. Anything less might mean that you've been kidding yourselves."

Ann and Mike were lucky. Waking up next to each other in the morning was an exhilarating experience for both of them.

For many of us, however, the chances of finding a partner who inspires that kind of exhilaration is relatively remote. The task of sifting through possible candidates for our romantic intentions is daunting.

Yet we continue to take risks, dating someone less than perfect, rationalizing our own intuitive sense of discomfort, in the attempt to find someone who matches our emotional, sexual, and intellectual needs. More often than not, we finally succeed, but not without the oftentimes excruciating pain of having to terminate one relationship after another until we are once again able to regain the sense of balance we may have lost during an unsuccessful coupling effort.

Ann went through two divorces and many romantic entanglements before she finally withdrew from the fray to restore her sense of dignity and self-esteem. Ending an affair of the heart can be a wretched and wrenching experience. The tighter the relationship, the more difficult it is. Couples who have spent time getting to know one another, who have become intimately acquainted with tiny bits of behavior—what makes each other giggle or respond sexually or smile knowingly—who have committed themselves to thoughts of a future with children and grandchildren have a very difficult time indeed. Yet, the de-structuring (destruction) of the relationship might be as necessary as life itself. When she chose to entertain thoughts about Mike, she was ready to take another chance on yet another man.

Intimacy

By the time we have reached the second stage of coupling, we have invested much time and emotional energy in the relationship. The decision to split up is no longer a matter of separating the wheat from the chaff or of picking out the contenders from the non-contenders. Largely, the decision centers on the degree to which we have begun to feel excluded from the intimacy we once shared with our partner.

When we feel we are making love *to*, rather than *with* someone, or that we are talking *to*, rather than *with* someone, the process of exclusion has already begun. If the exclusion/inclusion balance has become too distorted, the feelings of intimacy that once stabilized the relationship cannot do their job. At this point, either couples will seek counseling, hoping to rediscover the chemistry that brought them together in the first place, or they will seek an attorney to expedite the separation process.

Intimacy is a process of inclusion rather than exclusion. The process requires us to make a number of decisions simultaneously—most of them at an unconscious level.

We must decide, for example, whether to include our lover in our life script. We have our bit players and our leading women and men. For example, the cashier at the local market is a bit player: She requires little more than a nod in greeting and a "thank you" as we leave the store. It certainly would be unusual if we were to tell the cashier, the cab driver, or the newspaper boy our innermost secrets and desires. They are bit players, and their roles in our lives do not require that they know anything about us other than how they can serve us. Our boss, on the other hand, occupies a position of extreme importance. S/he is someone we may need to include at a deeper level, because our intimate thoughts, desires, and fears affect what happens out there in the work world.

The person we want most to include in our lives, of course, is our life partner. This is not quite as simple as it sounds: We might have several leading wo/men to

Connecting   57

consider, and we must then decide which one of these people fits the lover-for-life requirements.

Intimacy refers to the degree to which we allow people into our personal lives. Do we dare allow our lover into the deepest layers of our soul where he can see our faults and fears? Or, rather, do we feel more comfortable entertaining him in the foyer of our mind where more general issues are addressed (values, perceptions of the world order, choice of plays, music, etc.)?

The real question is whether we can trust our lover. Will s/he abandon us if we allow him to see our wounds from past relationships? Will s/he reject us if we reveal to him our unattractive habits and attitudes? Shall we allow him to romp freely through our minds and thoughts, letting him comfortably pamper us, argue with us, tease us, criticize us, or give us advice? On the other hand, are we more comfortable letting him visit the deepest layers of our personality on the condition that he be quiet and totally accepting?

We must also consider the time factor. For some of us intimacy is tolerable only on a time-limited basis: We want our lover to excite our senses and occupy our thoughts—on weekends and holidays. Allowing him into our life at the deepest levels may be OK, but only if we know that the encounter will end in a few days or a few months. Longer periods of closeness may trigger off feelings we do not enjoy—loss of control, boredom, etc.

Although they had successfully moved beyond Stage I, Ann and Mike were struggling with the process of becoming intimate, of deciding how deeply involved they wanted to become with each other. Ann needed to know what Mike was thinking and feeling, what his fears and desires were. Mike needed to be more private. He did not want to open up to Ann *all* the time.

When Ann and Mike entered the second stage of coupling, the stage where the boundaries between fantasy and reality became blurred, they had begun to examine the role each wanted the other to play. They had already decided whether the other person would a bit player or leading wo/man, how deeply they were willing to let the other person in, and how much freedom they were willing to allow each other to have.

Intimacy requires that we include others in our world. It requires that we share our perceptions and our experiences, our expectations and our beliefs, and, perhaps most importantly, our honesty. Our connection may be smooth or rough. However, it must be honest. With the honesty comes the recognition that both our lover and we exist as sentient beings. A relationship might exist without much passion and without much commitment, but few relationships will succeed without the kind of closeness and connectedness that comes with intimacy.

58 Couples at the Crossroad

Contact Boundaries

To understand fully what intimacy is all about, we have to understand the concept of *contact boundaries*. The contact boundary is the place where we leave off and the rest of the world begins. Everything on *this* side of my skin is me (mine, our), and everything else on *that* side of my skin belongs to you (the world).

When I sit in a chair and feel it pressing against my body, the point where I feel it becomes the contact boundary. There is contact at the skin level of my body. It is the place where I am separated *from* and yet connected *to* you (everything that is *not me*). If the chair is soft and yielding, the contact is a gentle one. If, on the other hand, the chair is hard and ungiving, the contact is less comfortable.

The boundary is the point at which we make contact with the outside world: the smell of flowers, the power of the sunset, the hardness of an angry look. It is the place where changes take place. It is the place where I can exchange the things in me for the things I need out there. For example, I can exchange the carbon dioxide in my lungs for the oxygen in the atmosphere; or I can exchange the happiness (sadness) in my heart for the warm and tender hug of a friend.

Contact boundaries can be OK, too rigid, or too loose. If the boundary is OK, I know who I am. I know what belongs to me and what belongs inside me (feelings, thoughts, and fantasies). With this knowledge, I can make constructive decisions about the world and my role in it. I know, for example, that my knowledge and my skills are my own, and I will not allow anyone to convince me that my work (thoughts, feelings) belong to them.

The contact boundary, however, can become too rigid. I may have decided at an early age that the world beyond the skin is dangerous. I then create an impermeable membrane between you (that is, everything outside my skin boundary) and me. I keep all my feelings and desires inside the thing I have come to know as me; I do not share my laughter or my anger or my sadness, because it is simply too unsafe. My early experiences might have taught me that to laugh or become openly angry would leave me vulnerable to criticism and/or abandonment. Nor will I allow your feelings and thoughts to enter my world. You, the world outside my skin, have become an alien world filled with demons I do not understand. My boundaries have become rigid. The result, of course, is the feeling of isolation and exclusion. Many people have survived the unyielding boundary. We regard them as recluses, iconoclasts, and tyrants.

If my boundaries are too loose, I become everything I see, hear, touch, or feel. I (con)fuse with the environment. If a murder is committed in France, I call the police and tell them I did it. If I am a schizophrenic, I see myself as part of the world (not *con*fused; simply *fused*): I am the lamp, the President of the United States, my father, or Jesus. I may believe my thoughts are being broadcast all over the world. What is inside me filters through a too permeable membrane: My rage, my impulses, my fears, and my desires are uncontrolled and uncontrollable.

Conversely, what is outside of my skin-boundary filters into my body. Your anger angers me; your fear frightens me; your impulses excite me. I have little control over the flow of my energy. My emotions do not know where to go, how to get there, or at what speed. My boundaries are too permeable, and reality becomes hazy. Because I have no clear idea of what is real and what is fantasy, I behave inappropriately.

The contact boundary, then, is like an aura, an energy field. If the field expands, the world outside my skin (including my lover) becomes part of me; if the energy field contracts, the world outside my skin (including my lover) is excluded.

If we are unhappy, pouty, sullen, emotionally withdrawn, or depressed, we recede to a place deep inside ourselves, making it difficult to maintain contact with the outside world and with each other. The greater the upset, the greater is the withdrawal. It is often at this point in the relationship we seek couples' counseling or individual psychotherapy. The major complaint, of course, is that there is "no communication"; that is, we no longer trust our partner with our thoughts and feelings—another way of saying, we no longer trust our partner to be *inside* us.

When, on the other hand, my lover and I are able to expand our contact boundaries at the same time, there is a merging of the love-energy fields, and, instead of two separate auras, we find one large one surrounding the two of us. We begin to experience each other in a different way; we experience "intimacy," a closeness born of shared boundaries and shared energies. Our boundaries dissolve. Rather than fearing "intrusion" or "abandonment," we freely enter and freely exit each other's mind, body, and soul. All judgment is suspended. We accept each other uncritically. We feel a deep sense of pride, beauty, and dignity.

Intrusion and Abandonment

Imagine that each of us swings on a pendulum. On one side of the pendulum lies the Fear of Intrusion. On the other side of the pendulum is the Fear of Abandonment. The pendulum swings between these two poles of emotional experience.

60   Couples at the Crossroad

Some swing more toward the Intrusion side; others, more toward the Abandonment side. Most of us tend to stay somewhere within a broad middle range.

The Intrusion-Abandonment phenomenon is particularly important because it affects the quality of our intimacy, our passion, and our commitment. When we swing toward the Intrusion side, we become nervous, panicky, or sometimes enraged; we sense someone is trespassing onto our emotional space. We become suspicious and querulous. We begin to show annoyance and irritability.

If we are relatively intact emotionally, we will begin to strengthen the boundaries to keep the intruder out. Sometimes, however, the boundary defenses are weak, and we find ourselves feeling paranoid. (The paranoid person is fearful of even minor intrusions, and he can become quite unmanageable when unwanted visitors, that is, *we* knock at the boundary door).

When we swing toward the Abandonment side, we sense that our lover is "leaving" us. The "abandonment," of course, often is not real. It usually stems from a distortion of an event. A slight criticism or an expression of dissatisfaction is all the ammunition we need to prove that others do not love us anymore. Our behavior then becomes childlike: We cling, we apologize, we manipulate by becoming "ill," or we pout. All of this has only one goal—to keep ourselves from feeling lonely and "abandoned."

Most of us will have a tendency to swing one way or the other; but not many of us can tolerate too many feelings of intrusiveness or too much abandonment. However, finding the place where we feel most comfortable is not easy. Some people swing wide and fast until they lose control. Histrionic and Bipolar patients often complain about their uncontrollable swings of emotions—emotions that include fear and rage.

The Abandonment/Intrusion themes resonated with Ann. While her early caregivers had never really abandoned her, she had become extremely dependent on her two ex-husbands. The more they attempted to establish some emotional breathing room, the more she clung to them. She simply had never learned to be on her own. Her mother had inadvertently taught her that depending on "your man" was what husbands really wanted, and her father never taught her otherwise.

Being alone was frightening to her. She could not imagine having no one there to help her with her everyday struggles. She had thought that she had learned to manage these feelings after her divorces, but now they seemed to be intruding into her relationship with Mike.

Mike responded the same way Ann's ex-husbands had responded. He experienced a sense of intrusion. He felt swallowed up on the one hand, and feelings of annoyance and anger on the other. He tried to establish a boundary—a comfortable emotional space—between Ann and him, and Ann experienced what she usually experienced: feelings of abandonment. The Intrusion/Abandonment pendulum was swinging wildly for each of them. However, they were in love, and love, time, and nature heal all.

The need for emotional and physical closeness is so strong that often we will imagine the feeling of "intimacy" even if there is no valid basis for it. This is especially true early in a relationship. During the contacting and connecting stages, erotic thoughts and sexy feelings are often misperceived and distorted. We treat them like whole realities when they are, in fact, merely reflections of the need for intimacy. Our boundaries become too permeable; we allow our desires to ebb and flow capriciously without regard for a more complete understanding of what is real. Sadly, we often discover, after committing ourselves to a particular notion of what the relationship is all about, we have merged with the wrong person at the wrong time.

The following statistics reveal the importance of intimacy and companionship:

- The death rate among widowed, divorced, and single people are significantly higher than for married people for both male and female populations between the ages of fifteen to sixty-four.

- Death rates for victims of cancer are significantly higher for unmarried people. The incidence of heart disease, cerebro-vascular disease, and hypertension is significantly higher for unmarried people than for married people. It appears that heartbreak occurs more frequently among unmarried people than among married people—literally as well as figuratively.

- The number of unmarried men who require institutionalization is 50 times higher than for married men. The ratio for unmarried women is 25:1.

- In the mid 1940s, scientists observed a number of foundling homes and orphanages. Orphans receiving regular attention, caressing, and cooing, grew and adapted fairly well. Children deprived of attention because of the high infant to caretaker ratio, or who were given only the barest of essentials, soon showed signs of a deep and unrelenting depression, later known as an "anaclitic" depression. They demonstrated little curiosity about, or alertness to, their surroundings. They became "failure to thrive" babies, and once they retreated into themselves, there was little chance they would ever recover. Rene Spitz, the physician attending these children, concluded that without companionship and consistent physical attention, "the spine shrivels" and the child is lost.

- Studies in England at the end of World War II sought to determine the effect of the Blitzkrieg bombing raids on young children. One of the interesting findings was that children, who were with their primary caretakers, generally their mothers, at the time of the raids, were able to get over the trauma. However, those children who were by themselves at the time of the bombings were traumatized beyond repair. Years later, even after intensive psychoanalysis, they continued to exhibit fear and anxiety disorders.

- Observations in medical facilities also provide dramatic insight into the power of human companionship. In one study, researchers found that the mere touch of a nurse's hand reduced a patient's heart rate by 30 beats per minute. In another study, two comatose patients responded to the touch of a human hand when no other stimulus could elicit changes in the patient's condition.

A sense of intimacy—a sense of oneness—relieves feelings of loneliness, and feelings of well-being emerge. It was no wonder, I had told Ann and Mike, that people will do virtually anything to find their mates.

6

Commitment

Having entered the second stage of coupling several months ago, Ann and Mike were now struggling with the whole notion of what commitment really meant, and why men seem to have so much trouble with it. Ann observed that once when she and Mike attended the wedding of a dear friend Mike seemed to get squirmy when the pastor used the words, "til death do you part." In his defense, Mike noted that his squirminess had nothing whatever to do with the words per se; he was reacting to the fact that the couple had already split up a half-dozen times and he doubted that death would be the only requisite for another break-up. Mike insisted that commitment was not difficult for him, but that finding a woman to commit himself to always had been. As Mike said this, he squeezed Ann's hand gently, and she seemed to understand that commitment might not be as much of a problem as she had once thought it might be.

Common lore holds that women are always ready to commit, but men need a bit of coaxing. Things have changed considerably in this regard. Women have become more independent and self-sufficient. Articles in popular women's magazines counsel readers about the new equality between men and women. They make cogent arguments for women's liberation. The notion of commitment has evolved from the full-time wife-stay-at-home-with-the-kids caricature into a free-wheeling, self-determined, empowered, I-have-a-right-to-be-happy caricature of womanhood. The problem with both of these stereotypes is that neither is real. Reality dictates that each of us negotiates the terms of our intimate relationships. Nowhere is this truer than in the degree and quality of our commitment to our lovers.

Men and women are willing to stay together for extended periods for three primary reasons: (1) companionship (2) "love" and (3) sexual fulfillment. What most of us want is a relationship based on friendship, mutual trust, mutual respect, and satisfying physical contact. Wo/men who have established a relationship based on these qualities have a better than even chance of making it to the

64   Couples at the Crossroad

altar—if that is the route they choose. Qualities that increase the odds include the ability to laugh, emotional balance, and a pleasing appearance.

Neither the boundaries of Intimacy, nor the sharp urgency of Passion accurately describe the third dimension of love—Commitment. Commitment in its most primitive form is *being* there; and, in its most refined aspect, it is being *there*. At first glance, it is hard to tell the difference; but there is a difference, and it is an important one.

Being there means that we "hang around." Neither intimacy nor passion is necessary. The coupling becomes a matter of convenience—whether it lasts for one night or fifty years.

Changing the emphasis from "*being* there" to "being *there*," with all its subtlety, makes for an entirely different experience between two people. We not only "hang around," we "hang around" in a particular way. We are devoted; we sit on the edge of our lover's boundary, always ready to step inside when invited, and always ready to withdraw when asked to do so. It is this devotion—this flexible attachment—that changes the relationship from a primitive, routine, spending-time-together to an energizing, joyful, and intimate event.

When commitment is lacking, we feel that we ourselves are lacking. Barriers to happiness spring up unannounced. Here are some of the things we sense intuitively:

- We do not communicate. We do not even attempt to solve problems together. The songster in the other tree responds to our song, but its song is empty of feeling and energy.

- We are mistrustful. The partner who wants and needs a "commitment" is guarded and vigilant, imagining (often with just reason!) that the sharing of feelings is limited by time. The partner unable to commit himself is also guarded because he does not want to leave the "wrong" impression—the impression he is going to be there for the duration. The dance can go on for years. (Of course, both people are aware of this within the first half-hour of the relationship, but are willing to play a long shot under the guise of patience.)

- We feel insecure and fear rejection. We do not know when "the other shoe will drop" but we are certain it will, and we keep looking for the signs.

- We feel the need for approval from the other person. Whether we are the high-commitment type or the low-commitment type, we become cautious. We do not want to offend the other's sensibilities. We choose our words cautiously, we behave cautiously, and we think cautiously.

Commitment   65

- We lose our flexibility (flex-ability), and we begin to act in a ritualized, highly predictable, cybernetic fashion. We follow one set of beliefs; it can be either our own or our partner's, but in either case the beliefs become rigid and inflexible. We behave the way we do for one reason: to avoid conflict and, unconsciously, to maintain the status quo. Problems continue to occur without solutions; and, ironically, solutions occur without consciously perceived problems.

- We strive for power and "I'm right-ness." Giving up even a tiny bit of emotional territory is tantamount to an admission of weakness and ineffectiveness. The high-commitment type wants to prove she is correct to want fidelity and devotion; the low-commitment type holds out for higher levels of dedication and loyalty. Neither truly understands that what the other wants is impossible.

- Ultimately, we experience a subdued but pervasive hostility that even high degrees of passion and intimacy can't erase. It comes out in the simplest transactions: what to buy, how much to spend at a restaurant, what kind of music is most civilized, whether the Republicans (Democrats) can ever truly represent the will of the people, etc.

Many of us have observed that this same kind of behavior follows a breakdown in the realms of Passion and Intimacy and we are, of course, correct. That is why a ripened love is three-dimensional. Each dimension can be independent of the other two, but in mature relationships, the three become the holy trinity of contentment.

In one of the most common compatibility profiles, a high-intimacy, high-passion couple meets and dates for a month or two until the partners discover that one of them is high on the Commitment dimension and the other is low on the Commitment dimension. If there is enough intimacy and passion, time and experience might bridge the gap between the two levels of commitment. Generally, however, this is not the case. Rather, the relationship begins to crumble slowly and resentment supplants affection.

Conversely, a relationship characterized by a high level of commitment and low levels of passion and intimacy produces the kind of predictability, stability, and sterility generally reserved for inmates serving long prison sentences.

I asked Ann and Mike to fill out a brief Commitment scale (see Item #8 on the Decision Index in the Appendix for the complete version of the scale). The lowest score either of them could receive on this brief test was 10; the highest score was 50. A score in the high range 40–50) suggested that they were in a relationship with someone whom they trusted, someone who was committed to you.

If the couple enjoyed a high degree of intimacy and passion, a moderate Commitment score (20–39) suggested that the relationship was a comfortable one. However, if insecurity and querulousness occurred frequently, it would not have bode well for the future.

Low scores (10 to 19) across the board would have implied the relationship was being held together by attributes other than commitment. This might work out for a while, but when things got tough, the brittleness of the relationship would have revealed itself. Of course, there have been instances when two passionate and intimate but uncommitted people get together with the explicit understanding that the relationship probably won't last forever. It is the exception rather than the rule, but for some people it works out just fine.

In the Ann's case, there was no score lower than a "3," suggesting that she was not experiencing any seriously disturbing feelings about her relationship with Mike. She did admit to early feelings of neediness, but as they became more comfortable with each other, the clingy feelings subsided.

Mike's ratings on the Commitment Scale were generally lower than Ann's scores. The only low score that really seemed to matter to Ann, however, was on item #8: "I find I worry a lot about what life will be like twenty years from now."

We spent the better part of a session discussing Mike's perception of a "committed" life. There were clear differences between the two people, Ann expressing complete confidence in a happy future and Mike expressing doubts about addressing the future when they could not even make decisions about the present! His responses to the other items fell within the average to high average range: He enjoyed his time with Ann, wanted to spend more time with her, and felt that she was willing to accommodate his need for attention. At times, feelings of dependency also bothered him, but these were manageable. There were no indications of grouchiness or lack of trust. In short, if Ann could tame Mike's apprehension about the future, it would be smooth sailing.

7

The Power of Moods

When we began counseling, Ann and Mike had four choices available to them: They could terminate the relationship, maintain it, expand it, or they could limit the time they spent with each other. Now that they had tentatively decided to expand it, they also needed to expand their education about themselves and about each other. Many decisions remained, amongst which was whether their mood cycles and life scripts were compatible.

On several occasions, Ann had pointed out that Mike could be grouchy and irritable. Mike in turn pointed out that Ann withdrew and seemed to be resentful whenever he left her. Ann admitted that although Mike and she were not living together, she became pouty when she saw him packing his bags after a wonderful weekend together. Changes in mood had become a major concern for each of them.

I explained the basic premise: We wake up in the morning, and we go to sleep at night. In between, we experience a stream of awareness, perceptions, emotions, and behaviors.

For example, "Going to Work" consists of a long series of activities that might include awakening at a particular time, performing multiple sub-activities such as showering, grooming, dressing, eating breakfast, riding to work and engaging in specific work activities, and then leaving for home.

These events flow simultaneously and sequentially from morning to night. Some of the events are planned; some are spontaneous. Sequences of behaviors, taken together, define what we call a "lifestyle."

We can apply the same idea to emotions. We wake up with an emotion, perhaps one left over from a dream or from an encounter the evening before. This emotion is followed by another emotion, which is followed by yet another, and so forth. Generally, these emotions are consistent with each other and with our overt behavior. If they are not, there is a problem. For instance, some angry people act "sweet," but intuitively we sense that they are seething. Some people laugh

68 Couples at the Crossroad

a bit too often, a bit too loudly, and then suddenly become sad and depressed. These people confuse us and put us on our guard.

How well our emotions flow along and correlate with the way we behave is important because significant discrepancies serve as danger signals. For example, angry feelings are often followed by withdrawal, disgust, resentment, and vindictiveness. If anger turns into rage and vindictiveness immediately, there is a real danger of emotional or physical assault. If a resentful person is unable to express his resentment directly, s/he may express it indirectly ("Oh, I'm sorry. I did not *mean* to step on your toe."), causing annoyance and avoidance. Most commonly, however, there is a natural resolution of feelings within a short period. The angry person expresses his anger in an appropriate and effective fashion; the resentful person finds a way of expressing his resentment more directly; and the depressed person screws up enough courage to fight off overwhelming discouragement and go on with life.

Several of the major mood chains are offered here as examples of how emotions change—or fail to change—over the course of time. Learning the subtleties of emotional change helped Ann and Mike examine dominant moods, mood sequences, and their influences on their relationship.

The Anger Sequence

The Anger Sequence begins with anger and then followed by a sequence of emotions: withdrawal, disgust, resentment, and vindictiveness. In the emotionally healthy person, the sequence resolves itself quickly and predictably. The most effective resolution comes in the form of the direct expression our anger. People who cannot express the anger directly may need to use unconscious adaptive maneuvers such as repression or denial—not the best way to resolve the problem, but often the only way under certain circumstances. For example, expressing our annoyance with our boss might not be in our best interest, so we have to swallow hard and subdue the emotion using whatever defenses we have available to us.

In many cases, however, the Anger Sequence does not resolve itself. We find ourselves ruminating about the event. Obsessive and Suspicious Thinkers carry the thoughts around with them day and night until they can figure out how shake them off. Impulsive Thinkers might take short cuts to resolution and simply act out their anger/rage without regard to consequence or propriety. Unfinished feelings demand completion: joy demands a feeling of light-heartedness, depression demands withdrawal, sadness demands tears, and anger demands physical and/or verbal release.

The Power of Moods 69

In the Anger Sequence, if the natural flow of feelings is blocked from completion, the sequence of emotions reverses itself. In the usual sequence, anger precedes withdrawal, which precedes disgust, which precedes resentment and vindictiveness. However, when the normal sequence is disrupted, the sequence of feelings reverses itself, and resentment/vindictiveness leads to disgust which leads to withdrawal and then to anger. Unless the sequence can be terminated, the sequence reverses itself repeatedly until through fatigue, distraction, or resolution, the sequence is abandoned.

Oddly, while much has been written about emotions, little has been written about the obvious fact that feelings follow a more or less prescribed course. Why one emotion follows another remains a mystery. On the one hand, the answer lies in each person's unique body chemistry and genetic make-up. On the other hand, a feeling such as withdrawal serves as a natural protective response to anger because (1) it protects us from further emotional disorganization (anxiety) and (2) it protects other people from the harmful effects of our temper outbursts.

Coming out of withdrawal, it makes a great deal of biological sense for a person to go into a short period of disgust, because with disgust comes a kind of emotional vomiting that helps the body rid itself of the initial toxic event (thought, picture, behavior). The emergence of resentment and vindictiveness appears to have some utility in that it allows us to keep the toxic event at arm's length until the matter is ready to be resolved. The Anger Sequence, then, goes something like this:

Anger → Withdrawal → Disgust → Resentment → Vindictiveness → (Resolution?)

So far, so good. The effective Anger Sequence works to discharge bad feelings and, to that extent, it has survival value. The question is whether the sequence is timely and consistent. By timely, we refer to the recession of feelings within a reasonable and "healthy" period; by consistent, we refer to the predictable sequencing of emotions each time the initial feeling (e.g. rage, anger, sadness, depression, euphoria) is fired off.

Problems with either the timeliness or the consistency of a mood chain will mean problems in a relationship. If we are unable to discharge feelings of anger or rage in a timely fashion, the chances we will end up being very unhappy. Verbal or physical violence and/or the wanton destruction of property may follow. Those of us who have not discovered a way to effectively discharge and resolve the Anger Sequence over an extended period often are the very same people who end up in prisons, hospitals, or in doctors' offices.

Each of us can be caught up in a particular phase of the Anger Sequence. If we become stuck in the "withdrawal" phase of the sequence, for instance, we will come across as depressed, unfeeling and uncommunicative. People will not be able to touch with either words or hugs, and may eventually give up the effort. Again, if the withdrawal phase persists for a long time, especially if the original triggering event took place when we were very young, the mood chain may lead to severe regression, the safety of hospitalization, or to life as a recluse.

Disgust, if protracted, may lead to cynicism, pessimism and malcontention. We experience "Disgusted" people as bitter and cynical people who dampen the spirit of fun and goodwill. They are "toxic" in the sense that we feel drained and tense even after a few minutes with them.

Likewise, if someone becomes fixated on resentment/vindictiveness, people around him walk away sensing something is "missing." The contact may be sharp, but the connection is weak, even though the resentful person wears a smile.

We want to emphasize that each of these emotions is not destructive in and of itself. Only when they fail to dissipate in a timely fashion, or when they become unpredictable do they cause problems for us and the people around us.

The Humiliation Sequence

As seen in the following sequence, Humiliation becomes troublesome because it is so closely tied up with shame and feelings of inferiority:

Humiliation/Shame/Inferiority → Fear → Hopelessness → Isolation → Agitation → Restlessness → Frustration → Anger → Withdrawal → Disgust → Resentment → Vindictiveness → (Resolution?)

This sequence may take many days, many months, or even years to resolve itself, because each emotion is so strong and so difficult to complete. The power of Humiliation/Shame/Inferiority is readily available to all of us. We need only to reach back to our experiences as a child: the first time we had a toileting accident or were caught with our hand in the proverbial cookie jar. Or, more meaningfully, as an adult, the time we made a fool of ourselves at the office party, or perhaps the time we exposed our thoughts, feelings, or nakedness to someone who rejected us outright, leaving us feeling too small to fight back.

The Power of Moods 71

Each emotion in this sequence plays a role in helping us regain our emotional equilibrium. We begin by feeling small and weak. We then become frightened and we try to distance ourselves from the humiliating person (event), or we try to appease him/her. Next comes a period of hopelessness: We do not know what to do so we withdraw and isolate ourselves. After a period in isolation, we begin the process of reintegration, the first stage of which is internal restlessness, experienced as irritation and agitation. This leads to attempts to change our situation, which in turn leads to feelings of frustration.

Frustration may lead to aggression, anger, or, if it is very great, to regression. Regression is the act of returning to a stage of behavior that has been "successful" in the past (tantrum behavior, poutiness, passivity). If we work through these emotional states, we experience growth. Moreover, that is what is most interesting. Without frustration, there is no growth. Ironically, if the frustration is too great, there also is no growth.

Infants fall down many times before they learn to walk. Kindergarten students learn to read only by making many mistakes and accepting correction. The temporary frustrations in both cases lead to growth. However, let's say we want a parent's attention, and our fictional parent can't or will not give us the attention we want no matter how much we ask, plead, or display our temper. We are then left with a hole in our personality—a blind spot—that prevents us from ripening into mature adults. Years later we may find ourselves sitting on the psychiatrist's sofa, wondering why we can't feel closer to our lover or spouse or children—or anyone else for that matter.

If the Humiliation/Shame/Inferiority Sequence is triggered many times before it is resolved, our perception of the world will be affected, and eventually the way we react to the people around us will be affected. Is it any wonder that wo/men in abusive (humiliating) relationships become so confused about who they are and what they need?

The destructive power behind feelings of shame and humiliation comes from our occasionally overwhelming sense of vulnerability. Invariably, our vulnerability in relationships is tested. Our soul mate fails a particular test: a birthday is forgotten, a tiny embarrassment in front of guests, a temper outburst when we've done something silly. If the pain of the disappointment is circumstantial, if it is not the product of malevolence, the emotional wounds heal, and the essential goodness of the relationship is reinforced.

Once the covenant of trust has been broken because of deliberate cruelty or abuse, however, the potential for hurt hangs over the relationship like the Sword of Damocles; the very essence of our love is negated and we become profoundly

72   Couples at the Crossroad

unhappy. The strain, the anger, and the pain infiltrate all aspects of our feelings of togetherness. Worst of all, we feel something akin to shame, a feeling that diminishes the likelihood that the situation can ever be entirely corrected.

Shame is a Band-Aid over an imaginary sore. We do not know where the sore is or what the sore looks like. However, we are scared to death that someone will yank that Band-Aid off and reveal the most hideous, the most repulsive something ever created. So we walk around protecting the Band-Aid, making sure no one gets close enough to peek underneath, or even to ask about it. We guard it and we pamper it, all the while feeling repelled by it. If we sense we can't protect the imagined blemish, we put yet another Band-Aid on top of the first one, and then add more until we are satisfied that no one will ever see what was never there in the first place!

Shame and accompanying feelings of humiliation need to be considered in terms of the "existential" positions of the parties involved. "Existential" in this case means the very essence of our relationship, not only with people but also with life itself. If we learn at an early (preverbal) age to think of ourselves as inferior (small, ugly, stupid, worthless, unacceptable), our vulnerability is very great indeed. Ironically, so is our willingness to forgive those who hurt us, because at a deep level we feel we deserve the abuse and the pain. We are willing to tolerate more than is healthy, because disappointment and abuse are consistent with the picture we have developed over many years.

Deep inside us lies a largely unknown but ubiquitous set of beliefs that serve as a backdrop for our decisions about our relationships and ourselves. These attitudes and values are so deeply ingrained into our character structure that we often have little direct awareness of them or control over them. They act as the vitamins of the mind: Without them, we cannot behave or think efficiently or realistically, yet most of us carry on our daily lives as though they weren't necessary at all.

Compatibility with our lover often reflects our compatibility with ourselves. To be compatible with ourselves we need to develop a benevolent set of beliefs about who we are, and about our purpose in life. If these beliefs are self-destructive or self-defeating, there is a high probability that they will be destructive and defeating to our relationships as well.

Our belief patterns, especially our beliefs about ourselves, our motivations, our expectations for the future, our notions about the direction our lives will take, govern the most important and yet the most subtle aspects of relationships. It is easy for people to tell us, based on what they interpret when they see us with our partners, that we are "incompatible." What people can't see, however—and what we ourselves often cannot see are the tiny cracks in our belief system, cracks revealing that the real problem in our relationships is not incompatibility with our partner or spouse, but rather our incompatibility with ourselves.

Our decisions about our lover are incontrovertibly linked to the picture/thoughts that make up our self-image(s) and our self-esteem. Clearly, if we feel competent, adequate, and beautiful inside, we respond to our lover's demands in a more joyous and forgiving manner. If we have doubts about our virility/femininity, or see ourselves as small and inferior, we respond to our lover's behavior and demands in a very different way.

Self-image refers to the way we see ourselves, the way we perceive ourselves inside our own minds. It is more complex than simple picture/thoughts because it involves our souls and our hearts. It involves us as sentient beings. It mirrors how we view our body, our intelligence, our behavior, and our attitude toward the world outside the skin-boundary and the people who inhabit it.

Self-image is often confused with self-esteem. However, the two are very different. Each of us has many self-images: I can see myself as a good father, a bad mountain climber and a better-than-average psychologist. Self-image is not an all-or-nothing deal. Our self-image differs according to the here-and-now situation in which we find ourselves.

Self-esteem is different. It is an assertion of our worth as human beings. It reflects a deep and pervasive decision we have made about ourselves. It reflects a true feeling that we have just before we fall to sleep at night, when the darkness acts as a truth serum that doesn't allow us to lie to ourselves—at least not until the next morning, when our psychological defenses are working again to protect us from painful thoughts and feelings.

We like ourselves and feel worthy, or we do not. Our level of self-esteem (respect, honor, love, and devotion) for ourselves does not really change—no matter what role we play in our life script. We may be able to subdue or repress our doubts for a short while, but in the end, we will have to make a declaration about our worth.

Fortunately, the unconscious mind and the psychological defenses we learned when we were children protect us against the overwhelming anxiety that comes with the realization that we may not feel particularly worthy or meaningful in this world. When these defenses break down, however, we suffer from terrifying nightmares, nervousness, and insecurity.

Self-esteem, then, is of primary importance. Without it, we can make few changes; and the changes we do make will not be permanent. Our self-image and our self-esteem work in tandem to draw up a viable blueprint for the changes we want to make.

How we think about ourselves today influences how we will behave tomorrow. If we have a poor self-image, and an equally short supply of self-esteem, our behavior in any given situation will reflect these picture/thoughts precisely. Self-confidence will be minimal; self-defeating behavior will dominate our relationships. Our involvement with our lover will drain us of energy and stamina. If we are predisposed to do so, we will drink more, abuse drugs more, eat more, or display more shoddy behavior.

The effects of a distorted self-image are pervasive. Every war has its casualties. The Vietnam War was particularly brutal. The weapons used by all sides of the conflict destroyed minds and bodies. Physicians at the Walter Reed Medical Center were called upon to perform an unusually high number of amputations. Many of their patients required extensive surgery.

Many men whose limbs had been amputated would experience pain and discomfort in the very same limbs that had been amputated weeks before! At night, these men would try to get out of bed only to discover they were legless. The body knew the limbs had been removed, but the self-image would not accept the fact. The image of a whole person had endured even though the reality had changed. This phenomenon, common among amputees, is called "Phantom Limb Pain."

The importance is this: We all suffer from "Phantom Pains" of one kind or another. It occurs not only when limbs are removed but also when we experience emotional damage. Humiliation, embarrassment, and feelings of helplessness that all of us have experienced may no longer exist. Yet we behave as though they do. All of us have felt rejected, teased, and left out. We were too young and small to understand, but the memories linger. The events now are mere picture memories, but we walk around feeling the same feelings of rejection and isolation we felt many years before. These experiences have been etched into our unconscious minds until we have lost sight of what is real: We are reacting to past life events as though they are a present reality.

Can you imagine how this affects our relationships? We bring a troubling past into a relationship where it plays no useful role. Psychoanalysts call this phenomenon "transference." Most of us are unaware of the transference phenomenon; yet it is there, evoking behaviors that disrupt the smooth flow of caring for our lover.

Here is a Phantom Limb exercise designed to increase awareness of early memories that may have altered Ann's and Mike's perception of themselves and of each other. I asked them to do the following:

List any "Phantom Pains" resulting from early experiences that may interfere with your relationship with Mike (Ann). For example, if you were teased as a youngster because of your weight—appearance, speech, compulsions—how do these memories affect you?

Ann's response:

"Looking back to my childhood, I can see where I might have a lot of the 'Phantom Pain' we talked about. For example, I can remember my mother always doing things for me. I do not think I ever even made a bed or darned a sock. She always seemed to look at me as though I was disabled—or at least as though I was incompetent. I am sure she thought she was doing what she felt was best, but it left a scar. I still catch myself even after all of these years wondering whether I can really do things for myself or whether I'm some kind of imposter who's getting away with something. It is really a stupid thought. I've borne children, raised a family, paid my bills, and published three best selling books! And I still wonder whether any of it is real or whether my mother was right. As far as its influence on our relationship, I think it has very definite effects—all bad. I keep wondering whether Mike will wake up next to me one morning and see the thing I grew up believing I was—an incompetent, ditzy blonde. It puts me on my guard and it makes me resentful. Poor Mike doesn't even realize what I'm angry about most of the time. He just shrugs and lets the emotional storm pass. The worse part of it is that there really isn't anything he can do about it, even if he did know what I was upset about. It's a no win situation for him. If he says, 'Do not worry about it...I'm here for you...let me take over some of the stress for you', it makes me feel more incompetent. If he doesn't say any of those things, I begin to think that he's seeing through the façade and that he's ready to dump me. It's all very confusing."

Mike's response:

"I had no idea you felt like that! However, you are right. I do not think there really is anything I can say or do to comfort you. Lord knows I have tried! (Ann laughs.) But, just so you get it straight: I love you very much and it'll take more than a petty annoyance to drive me away. (Tears run freely from Ann's eyes.)

Getting back to my 'Phantom Pains', I have carried around the thought that I cannot get close to people the way I would like to. The thought is like a splinter, it hurt so much. I've tried for years to get into groupie things, encounter groups, sensitivity training groups, and those kinds of group experiences, and I always walk away feeling emptier than I did before. I'm not sure where I got the 'empty'

76   Couples at the Crossroad

feeling. I think it may have been the emphasis both of my parents put on brainy activities. Instead of enjoying a day at the beach, picnicking, or going fishing, we spent the day attending lectures or doing crossword puzzles. The message I got was that I was a self-contained human who did not need anybody else. Certainly, it made sense.

I know my parents adored me, but I do not think I could ever count on them to 'depend' on each other or me. Everyone just did his own thing, and I grew up with a fierce sense of self-sufficiency, which even now interferes with my relationship with Ann. I think that's why I have such a low score on that intimacy scale we completed before. It's not for lack of love. It's more like a lack of getting outside my own thoughts. I guess the real irony is that I grew up exactly the way my parents wanted me to, and now I treat Ann the same way my father and mother treated each other." (Ann holds Mike's hand and squeezes gently.)

If we suffer from a low self-esteem because of real or imagined rejection by our earliest caretakers, there is a better than even chance that our relationship will never ripen fully—although we might pretend otherwise. Often we will kiss and make up, only to be deluged with not-always conscious feelings of suspiciousness, helplessness, and rage, followed in short order by the re-entry into the "what's next" emotional lottery we've come to expect.

The Failure Sequence

Here is another sequence, the Failure Sequence, all too common among couples who complain of failed attempts at establishing personal relationships:

Feelings of Failure → Feelings of Self-Denigration → Isolation → (Resolution?)

The Failure Sequence begins with the feeling we have somehow disappointed someone. We perceive ourselves as inadequate and incompetent. If these feelings are turned inward, there is self-denigration, depression, and withdrawal. Of course, the feelings can be turned outward as well, and, instead of we ourselves feeling small and incompetent, we project the "holes" in our personality onto the environment (most often the people we love or the people we hate). If incompetence is one of those "holes," we begin to see "incompetence" in our lover, our boss, our best friend, our worst enemy, or anyone else who has absorbed our interest. It is they who are inept, not we. If this kind of thinking is carried to an

The Power of Moods   77

extreme, we begin to develop delusions about our power vis á vis the power of the people around us. Suspicious thinking follows in short order.

Depending on the nature of our (or our lover's) personality structure, failure will trigger either subtle forms of panic/resignation or temper/rage. The resolution in either case requires a realistic assessment of who we are, what our weaknesses are, and what we can do about them. If we are able to overcome the failure and the resulting frustration, we become stronger; we become the heroes of life. If we are not able to overcome the failure, we (and our lover) will become increasingly more withdrawn or tempestuous, and—more often than not—dour, defensive, and combative.

The Addiction Sequence

This chapter would not be complete without a consideration of another sequence, the Addiction Sequence, an increasingly common condition in which the "love addict" finds the relationship burdensome and self-destructive, yet feels powerless to end it. To say that the addicted partner "loves too much" is a simplification of the real problem, which may be that s/he does not know how to love at all.

A mature love relationship, by definition, requires reciprocity. We give and we receive according to our energy and our needs, but always there is a mutually agreed upon give and take. In the case of an addictive love, the relationship swings rapidly and erratically; the see-saw affection is never quite balanced, and frustration, panic, and anger displace the playful, mildly exhilarating, smoothly coordinated exchanges of passion and intimacy we have come to expect in healthy relationships.

The Addiction Sequence is particularly difficult because, despite the pain, the addicted lover does not want to give it up. She denies, she represses, and she rationalizes. In short, she does whatever she has to do to push distress out of conscious awareness. Invariably, with time, the relationship becomes worse: tension and stress increase; satisfaction and happiness decrease.

Nonetheless, the addict of love holds onto her relationship with the tenacity of a child who senses she is about to be abandoned. Catastrophic expectations set off a chain reaction of behaviors and moods that have the same intensity we find in the alarming behavior of alcoholics and drug addicts who have been cut off from their supplies. The destructive nature of the addiction becomes apparent as we consider the ongoing, increasingly debilitated condition of the addict over time.

Comparisons between an addictive process and a disease process are common; and they are not without foundation.

Love addicts learn their lessons from unhealthy family relationships long before a particular "love" relationship actually begins. The sequence seems to begin innocently enough when the addict is asked to assume too much responsibility for the happiness or contentment of a chronically ill member of her family, often an alcoholic parent. The responsibility calls for total control over a situation where total control is impossible. With the investment of time and energy, a state of dependency develops, and, after many years, becomes crystallized. The question, of course, is who becomes dependent on whom?

The answer is that the caretaker (addict) and the patient (family member) depend on the other. A symbiotic relationship has been created: One cannot exist without the other without severely damaging the by-now-accepted delicate balance within the relationship. The result of this misaligned alliance is a skewed view of the world and, more relevant, a skewed view of love relationships.

The love addict either creates—or searches for—a relationship that mimics what s/he has become accustomed to: a relationship with a dependent, unhappy, and needy wo/man. Perversely, the key to the relationship is not "being happy," or "being adored," or "being comfortable." The key to the relationship is trying—trying to please, trying to cure, and trying to control. The addiction is not to love per se, or even to the other person: the addiction is to the feeling that historically came along with love, a feeling called trying.

Here, then, is the Addiction Sequence:

Need For Control ("Tries" To Love, "Tries" To Keep Lover Happy) → (Guilt/Anger/Frustration ("Tries" To Control-Again) → ("Tries To Talk About It" (Guilt/Anger/Frustration) → Feelings Of Failure (Excuses To Friends And Family → Withdrawal (Irrational Fears And Anger) → Obsession With Control → Failure → Attempts To Escape (Becomes Workaholic, Alcoholic, Drug Addict And/Or Suicidal) → Bottoms Out (Admits Defeat) → Seeks Help (AA, Group Therapy) → (Rebirth Of Own Interests And Spontaneity)

The Addiction Sequence is a complicated and an extremely long sequence. It takes many months and perhaps many years to complete. Many addicts never complete it. In essence, it begins with the need for control (a need that is foisted upon the addict) and ends with rebirth (a need generated by the will to survive). "Trying" to make the partner happy leads to "trying" to control, then to "guilt/

frustration/anger," which then leads to obsessive "need to control", and to self-destruction or (hopefully) rebirth.

It is difficult to find any room for relief in such a sequence of behaviors and moods. The love addict struggles to establish equilibrium within herself as well as between herself and her lover. Failure to achieve a proper balance produces a protracted state of emotional crisis in both parties.

Mood Chains in Real Life

Ann and Mike seemed to be doing well. They freely discussed their concerns about the future and the role of moods. They reported that in the early spring, they had spent three days together on Plum Island, a small island off the north shore of Massachusetts. The days were filled with walks on the beach, the evenings with loving and laughing. However, when it was time for Ann's return to Boston and for Mike's return to England, each began to go through a series of moods.

Ann recalled that the drive to back to Boston seemed to take forever. She had felt an odd mixture of exhilaration and sadness, excitement mixed with fear. Mike, she observed, was quiet. For his part, Mike recalled that he and Ann were both experiencing a sense of profound loss.

As Ann recounted the story, she noted that about twenty miles from Boston, she suddenly felt insecure. She asked, "Where do we go from here, Mike? You know I loved the time we spent together. You seem so quiet, so detached—have I done anything wrong?" Mike did not respond at all, and Ann began to think that Mike hadn't heard a thing she had said.

Ann laughed as she recalled thinking, "Typical male!"

Her voiced softened as she remembered Mike turning to her and, placing his hand over hers and squeezing it gently, said, "Ann, I love you very much."

Ann's hurt dissolved. In its place came confusion. What was she supposed to say now? She decided to remain quiet and to let Mike lead the conversation.

The farmland surrounding their Newburyport hideaway gave way to the tree-lined highways, to the ubiquitous shopping centers, and then, finally, to the sky-scrapers of Boston. Mike had remained quiet throughout the fifty-minute drive, and Ann had let him keep his emotional distance, telling herself that his behavior was sadness cloaked with aloofness.

I asked Ann and Mike if they could spot the changes in each other's moods as time wore on. Ann responded that she had seen Mike's visage change with each mile. First, there was withdrawal, then she saw his mouth turned down at the corners, and then his eyebrows arched. Then there was a sigh, and then he touched her hand again. Each emotion lasted only a minute or two and then merged imperceptibly into the next one. The sequence was completed by the time they reached Ann's condominium in Boston. Despite Mike's silence, Ann recalled how deeply touched she was by his gentleness and the feeling of sadness she (correctly) guessed troubled Mike as he prepared for his trip across the Atlantic.

Mike reported that the emptiness of the apartment was palpable. Ann's sons hadn't yet returned from the visit with their father. He could no longer hide behind the isn't-the-landscape-beautiful as an excuse for the lack of conversation.

Ann remembered pouring two drinks, and, handing him one of them, she sat down next to him. She remembered thinking that Mike's eyes seemed to have lost their sparkle. "Mike," she said gently, "what's wrong…what are you thinking?"

Then—as Ann recalled the incident—the most romantic scene unfolded before her. Mike looked into her eyes. He smiled the same smile Ann saw the first time they had met. "Ann," she remembered him saying, "what is wrong is I do not want to leave you now or ever." He sipped his drink, never letting his eyes wander from her. "I need to hear you say that you will marry me as soon as I can settle my affairs back home."

She had waited months to hear these words, but now that it happened, she was confused. She told him, "Mike, I want that more than anything. Are you sure? We haven't spent a lot of time together. Don't you think we need to wait?"

Mike remembered his response to her: "No, I do not think we should wait. I love you and I want to spend the rest of my life with you."

I urged Ann to remember the changes in her mood just as she clearly remembered the minute changes in Mike's mood.

"My breathing quickened and my heart began to pound. I was becoming very confused and nervous. I wondered: What is this feeling I'm feeling right now? Was it love? Panic? Perhaps both!"

What Ann felt was (con)fusion. Telling where one feeling left off and the next began was difficult.

This is truer for some mood sequences than for others. For example, the Humiliation sequence clusters feelings of humiliation, shame, and inferiority together, and while we experience each of these feelings differently, the differences are subtle and hard to define. The other components of the sequence however are relatively easy to spot: fear and hopelessness along with liberal doses of isolation, agitation, frustration and anger. At the end of the sequence, we gener-

The Power of Moods   81

ally find feelings of resentment and vindictiveness, often not expressed because of the very first feelings of the sequence, that is, inferiority and shame.

To dramatize this point, I asked Ann to recall her first marriage, a time when she had experienced, by her own admission, extreme feelings of inferiority. Tentatively, she remembered how her husband let her know indirectly—and sometimes not so indirectly—how dependent and silly she was. By the end of the first year of marriage, she became frightened, discouraged, hopeless, and finally ended up barricading herself for days at a time in her bedroom. (They slept in separate bedrooms because, as her husband was sure to tell her on a regular basis, there was no need to sleep together if she couldn't handle the simple act of sexual gratification.)

After months of emotional bashing, Ann became increasingly agitated and frustrated. She still had enough of her self-esteem left intact to know that she could not go on this way. At first, she began to show her anger passively: She neglected the wash, the cooking and the housekeeping for days on end. However, her attempts to express her anger left her feeling so helpless, she withdrew even more.

Looking back on it, she recalled feeling that she had to isolate herself almost completely to keep from committing acts of violence either to her husband, to herself, or to both. However, she learned something crucial during this period. Her feelings, however nasty they were, would pass if given enough time and if she had the courage to seek assistance.

She also learned that her feelings of shame and inferiority were reflections of old emotions learned at home before she could walk or talk. It was now time that she re-decide those early decisions about her worthiness, to learn how to become aware of her feelings of anger and frustration and withdrawal, and to accept them knowing that they would pass in time.

The last words Ann had heard from her estranged husband after their divorce was, "But why didn't you tell me?" Ann laughed as she recalled how completely out of touch her husband had been. "Not that he was a bad man," she told Mike and me, "he was just so self-absorbed. And that's why it's so important for me to know that Mike's trouble with commitment won't turn me into an emotional vegetable again."

Mike's response? He picked up Ann's hand and kissed it gently, all the while looking so deeply into her eyes that she actually began to swoon.

While all moods have beginning points and ending points, the Anger, Humiliation, Failure, and Addictive Sequences appear to be the ones with the most potential for harming our relationships.

82 Couples at the Crossroad

The Flow of Emotions

Emotions follow a specified course that, under normal circumstances, is relatively permanent. We only need to study the sequence and the duration of our lover's mood phases to get a rough idea of how life will be in the future. If, for example, our lover becomes enraged, and this mood lasts for three days before slipping into withdrawal, the chances are that this will be the mood pattern in the future.

It takes a certain amount of patience, stamina, and generosity to tolerate three days of anger/rage. Our job, of course, is to discover whether we can realistically handle this kind of emotional reactivity on our lover's part. Clearly, our assessment should include a consideration of our own mood, and the sequences they follow: How do we respond to our lover's anger/rage/withdrawal? How long does it take us to run through *our own* mood chains?

Mood Duration and Quality

Each person's unique biology and early teachings limit the number and quality of mood sequences. Some people are more complicated than others. Conversely, some people seem to experience few emotions or moods. In either case, biological make-up and genetic disposition appear to play major roles in the production of mood sequences; early teachings account for the rest.

How we feel and behave influence the behavior of the people around us. For example, the behavior of children who do not seem to have the "genes" for remorse will elicit more intense discipline from frustrated and frightened parents than the behavior of children who are more compliant. Likewise, research tells us that "neurotic" people experience stress for longer periods than do "normal" people do. In one study, for example, a group of neurotic individuals and a group of normal people were compared on a number of physiological measures. Both groups were exposed to the sound of a gunshot. While both groups reacted immediately and intensely to the noise, the neurotic group took much longer to return to a normal baseline of physiological reactivity. Other studies strongly suggest that our reaction to stress is influenced by genetic predisposition.

Uniqueness of Mood Sequences

Each mood follows a standard course, which differs from person to person in intensity and quality. When you think back to your experiences with old friends, family, and lovers, you can begin to appreciate that each person has a certain "personality" that makes him different from others. For some people, an angry feeling is followed by withdrawal; for others, it is followed by a disquieting calm. For still others, it is followed by a temper outburst, quickly resolved and quickly forgotten. Each of us differs in the way our feelings evolve and finally resolve themselves. The sequence of emotions is our own in terms of duration and quality.

Disruption of Mood Phases

Catching someone in one of the moods of an extended mood chain often leads to an exacerbation of the mood. Blocking the angry feeling leads to more anger; blocking the feeling of withdrawal leads to more withdrawal; and blocking the feeling of humiliation leads to even more humiliation. Each feeling has a prescribed course and duration, and we have to respect them. We need to be patient; each person needs time to complete his sequence of feelings. The natural occurrence of events needs to flow freely. This requires we understand how people operate and how not to take it personally when we inadvertently interfere with the resolution of a sequence of emotions.

The interruption of a mood sequence leads to behavior reflecting the nature of the blocked mood as well as a general feeling of "incompleteness." We have all experienced "saying the wrong thing at the wrong time." Someone we care about (and perhaps love) is angry, and we try to be helpful by being clever or witty. The next thing we know there is a blast of cold air that sends us cowering to the next room. We call our best friend and ask, "What did I do wrong?" Our friend, if he is wise, says, "Do not worry. You just caught her at a bad time. It'll blow over. Just give it time." Similarly, with kindness and affection, we may say to the person caught up in one of the phases of the Humiliation/Shame/Inferiority Sequence, "It's not your fault, you just did what you thought was right." The person, instead of feeling relieved, becomes even more withdrawn, and even more isolated.

Each mood or sequence may be slowed or quickened through therapeutic intervention, but the sequence itself follows a prescribed course. By "therapeutic intervention," we do not mean psychotherapy. A therapeutic intervention could be a vacation, the adoring arms of a son or daughter around our waists, a call from an old friend, or an act of kindness by a stranger. Disgust melts with honesty and truth. Anger dissipates with affection. Humiliation is lessened with self-forgiveness. The sequence of emotions still runs its course, but the course is shortened, often dramatically so.

Feelings of Well-being

We subjectively experience free flowing mood chains as feelings of well being and self-control. When we block the natural flow of emotions (or allow our lover to do so) we feel tense and unfulfilled. The blockage of a mood chain produces frustration and feelings of being "unfinished"; and this leads to an irrepressible desire to complete the emotional sequence finally. On the other hand, when we execute the sequence completely, we return to a feeling of completion. We have taken care of the "unfinished business," and we feel whole again.

Feelings Don't Last Forever

Our ability to predict a sequence of behaviors or feelings provides us with consistency and with a certain degree of control, both of which make difficult emotional encounters tolerable. We often say that someone is a "grouch" or "depressed" or "bitter." What we do not seem to understand too well is that these mood states do not last forever, although they can dominate the emotional life of some people for hours, days, or, in unusual instances, even for months and years. There are individuals who cannot (biologically) or who will not (psychologically) relinquish certain moods, and who remain fixed permanently in a particular emotional state.

If we could understand mood sequences, we could better appreciate that there are times when it is better to keep our mouths shut rather than to barge in on his privacy. In short, we need learn to be patient, to be watchful, and to learn what kinds of behavior to expect when we inadvertently stumble into a particularly nasty mood phase.

To their credit Ann and Mike were committed to the task and eventually learned how to deal with each other's moods. Had Ann, after much effort and goodwill, failed to find a satisfying response to Mike's sensitivity or aloofness, she might have had to confront the possibility that the coupling process would not ripen. If she couldn't find an effective way of dealing with Mike's mood changes, she would have had to limit or terminate their relationship before she found herself having to deal with her own perennial destructive mood sequence—the one triggered by the feelings of failure, shame, and humiliation.

Emotional Death

The blockage in a particular mood sequence is experienced as "numbness," "emotional death," or "dread" (Angst). Mood chains are made up of different moods that merge imperceptibly into each other until an emotional sequence is completed. This requires a flowing of energy. When the flow of energy is blocked or interrupted, we experience an "emotional death" or numbness. We need only to recall a time when we became immobilized by trauma to realize how strongly such a blockage affects us. Subjectively, we feel an all-pervasive sense of dread—a combined state of paralysis and panic.

For example, if an Anger Sequence is triggered by a betrayal of someone we love, the normal sequence of moods includes anger, withdrawal, disgust, resentment, and vindictiveness and the resolution. Getting to the point of the resolution, however, requires that we work through the anger and the other disruptive emotions. If we fail to sense movement or progress, we begin to experience emotional stupefaction; and we begin to dread the future. The dread—panic plus paralysis—colors our perception of everything around us. The world is not safe; wo/men cannot yet be trusted; we become hyper-vigilant, suspicious, and easily startled. We interpret our environment through a filter made up of blocked emotions and numbness. We cannot free ourselves to enter a new relationship because we have not yet completed the last one.

Acts of Destruction

If a blocked emotion can't be loosened up through our own natural ability to reorganize our affective (emotional) life or through the interventions of a change agent (psychotherapist, physician, clergy, son/daughter, lover, change of environment), the internal numbness we feel may very well be expressed externally through acts of self-destruction, or, in some cases, through violence. This is one of the reasons why involvement with someone on the "rebound,"—someone who has not fully worked through feelings of loss—is emotionally so dangerous. Those of us who are sensitive to feelings of rejection vow never to get involved with such people.

Of course, there is another perspective: We can appreciate the nature of our candidate-lover's dilemma, give him time, and make auspicious interventions of kindness, concern, and attention. If, despite our good intentions, our lover continues to remain "numb," it is perhaps best to part—at least for a while—and to allow the emotional forces to continue to unfold in their own fashion. The rule of

86   Couples at the Crossroad

thumb is this: Provide gentle encouragement twenty times—the normal rate for learning. If our lover does not "get it," we need to free ourselves to look elsewhere, and to free our lover so he can work through the blocked feelings.

Feelings of Confusion

The feeling we call "confusion" is the result of several incongruous mood sequences fired off simultaneously. This is most apparent in abusive relationships or in situations where there is "co-dependency." If our lover were consistently mean-spirited, destructive, and deceptive, we could respond with clear and pure anger. The matter would be resolved quite quickly. We are tripped up, however, because often in addition to anger our lover evokes some other feeling—concern, caring or sweetness. We find ourselves feeling confused instead of angry (although the reasons for our anger are reasonable).

This may be a sign that our lover is a skillful manipulator of feelings and thoughts. More often, however, the confusion erupts because he presents a genuinely mixed picture of behaviors: nastiness/destructiveness/hurtfulness plus sweetness/carelessness/ignorance. Part of us responds with the anger/rage sequence; another part responds with a caring/love sequence of emotions. We feel confused because we are confused. The emotional sequences are incompatible; our bodies reflect the incompatibility with tears and clenched fists; our minds reflect the incompatibility with confusion.

Confusion is a signal that there is something very wrong with the emotional exchange between our lover and us. If it occurs too often, it augers ill for the future, and it is best not to linger.

Like Ann and Mike, we all need to (re)learn how people experience their feelings. Ann, when confronted with a withdrawn Mike, let the situation ride until a more propitious moment arrived. Mike was less sensitive to Ann's moods, but he appreciated her efforts to make contact with him. This was the very essence of the coupling process: to train each other within a sphere of comfort and safety.

Ann's feelings of nervousness and Mike's longing to be with her had propelled them into a mad dash for counseling. Their feelings were powerful and needed to be resolved before the final step—marriage—could be taken. Again, they reassured me that they truly loved each other and they were convinced that working on the issues centering on intimacy would not take long. I believed them. However, I also realized that they needed to make other decisions. It was time to explore the self-system.

8

Assuming Control

Contact boundaries define the psychological location of the I-Thou relationship. Whatever is on *this* side of my skin is *me*; whatever is on the *other* side of my skin belongs to *you*—the world outside of me. Self-control in many ways reflects our success with establishing those boundaries because it involves an appreciation of the difference between our inner world and our outer world. The world inside us consists of our feelings, senses, and behaviors; the world outside consists of people, the environment, and the "objective" experiences people share. We are self-controlled when we have learned how to assume responsibility for the experiences—behaviors, feelings, and sensations—that actually belong to us.

We say we are in control when we remain calm under stress. In reality, what we often mean is that we know the difference between external pressures and our internal strengths, and we can keep the external stresses outside us—where they belong.

Our awareness of this difference determines to a large degree whether we are successful in personal relationships. People who allow external pressures to get to them, who give up when adversity strikes, who, in short, let things "happen to them," lose *self*-control, and become victims of *other*-control.

Like it or not, all of us are engaged in directing the life script we wrote long ago. Those of us who have self-control not only direct that play; we produce it, write it, and serve as its casting agent. Our control lies largely in our having the power to hire and to fire the other actors in our life play, and in our ability to populate our world with whomever we choose. We can fill it with ogres and witches, or we can find the people with whom we can harmonize while we follow our own chosen paths. What we decide to do, of course, depends on our willingness to set the boundaries, and to make a clear statement about what we want, and what we need as sentient beings.

Achieving self-control in relationships often means making not-so-easy changes, changes that require a rethinking of who we are, and what we want out

88   Couples at the Crossroad

of life: changes in attitude, in behavior, and in the values we have carried around with us for many years. The alternative to us changing ourselves is allowing others to change us. For example, we can let our parents change us, or we can leave that responsibility to astrologists, to psychologists, to religious leaders, and even to our lover.

If we let others—including our lover—assume the responsibility for us, we can be free of blame if anything goes wrong. The price we pay, however, may be too steep: We lose *self*-control—the control to direct our lives as we see fit. We end up feeling victimized and cheated of our independence. Ultimately, we begin to feel like phonies. Nothing is real—neither our successes, nor our failures. Moreover, since we cannot assume responsibility for them, we end up feeling unreal, too. That indeed is a bad feeling to carry around with us.

Self-motivation and self-direction demand that we *make* things happen. They activate an inner drive that insists we accomplish exactly what we want to accomplish, and to persist and to persevere no matter how discouraged we become.

Dominant thoughts—and their accompanying fantasies—move us in their direction just as surely as the wind moves a sailboat along its path. If these dominant thoughts are positive, they move us in a positive direction. If these dominant thoughts are negative, they move us in a negative direction. Positive, in this case, means healthy, growth producing, and empowering. Negative, on the other hand, means unhealthy, stunting, and dissipating. In short, without self-motivation and self-direction, we cannot expect to recognize the "path with a heart."

Dominant thoughts dictate largely what the future holds for us (and for our lover). If we are constantly angry or disappointed in our relationships, our behavior reflects this attitude; if we are happy and grateful, our behavior will reflect this attitude precisely.

As a measure of their dominant thoughts, I asked Ann and Mike to do the following exercise:

List as many personal goals as you can think of in exactly two minutes. Next to each item on your list, indicate whether the goal will take one month, six months, one year, or five years to accomplish. To the right of each item, indicate whether your level of optimism and your self-image will allow you to reach each goal (rate your optimism: 1=very optimistic, 2=somewhat optimistic, 3= not very optimistic). Finally, how does Mike (Ann) help or hinder progress?"

Ann's responses:
To write a successful novel—12 months—2 (somewhat optimistic)

Assuming Control   89

To settle down with Mike—2 years—1 (very optimistic)

To enroll my eldest son in college—one year—1 (very optimistic)

To lose 10 pounds—6 months—3 (not very optimistic)

"Mike really can't help me with my writing, except by doing what he's always done—letting me have me have my space and giving me a hug when I get discouraged. I've never really tried writing a full novel before and the prospect is daunting, but optimistic—sort of.

"Settling down with Mike is the most important of all my goals. That's really why we're here—so we can get help in understanding why two people who love each other as much as we do hesitate for even a minute. I think we're getting closer though and I expect that we'll be able to resolve whatever problems we might have sooner than we thought. (Ann looks expectantly at Mike, who returns her gaze with a small but approving smile.) I put two years next to that goal but I do not really think it's going to take that long.

"Getting my eldest son enrolled in a good college is another goal I have. I can't imagine he'll have any problem grade-wise, but I'll have to sell a lot of children's books to supplement any financial assistance we might receive. I'm optimistic about it. Mike told us he would help if we wanted him to, and, although I might feel funny about it, I'll take him up on it if money becomes a problem. Education is very highly regarded in our family, and I would work three jobs if I had to just to make sure Jason gets a fair start in life.

"My last goal is losing ten pounds. But really I've had that particular goal since my Junior year in college, and I do not expect that I'll be any more successful this year than I was back then. Mike could help a lot by refusing to take me out to nice restaurants or bringing us beautiful desserts from the Italian Bakery up the street. Y'know, I've changed my mind. Let's get rid of that goal. It's just too silly. (Ann smiles broadly, and Mike laughs)."

Mike's responses:

To get a job transfer to the United States so that I can be closer to Ann and the children—6 months—1 (very optimistic)

To develop an interest in a hobby that Ann and I can share—2 years—1 (very optimistic)

To join the staff of one of the local Universities, either Boston College, MIT or Harvard, as an adjunct professor and teach a course in political history—2 years—2 (somewhat optimistic)

To successfully complete the Boston Marathon—1 year—3 (not optimistic)

To become part of Ann's family as husband and father to her two children—1 year—1 (very optimistic)

90   Couples at the Crossroad

"Getting a job transfer to the United States won't be difficult. I've already discussed the matter with my supervisor who understands my situation completely. As a matter of fact, my company plans to open a branch office here in Boston and I have been asked to head it up, so I am totally optimistic about my future here.

"Finding a hobby to share with Ann won't be too difficult either. We both like golf, scuba diving, fly-fishing, and gardening. My objective is not so much to find a mutual interest but really to find time to share. It doesn't really matter what the activity is.

"Becoming part of the staff at one of the local universities will be difficult, I think, mostly because Boston produces so many bright minds and so many politically sophisticated people who know politicians who know the Dean or the Dean's wife or the Dean's cousin, etc. As I get the lay of the land, perhaps I'll learn how to charm someone with influence at one of the schools. It has been a lifelong dream of mine to engage bright students in the political process. However, I am not very optimistic at this point.

"Nor am I optimistic about running the Boston Marathon next year. The most I've ever run is about 15 kilometers and I do not train as much as I would need to in order to complete the 26-mile course. But, again, it has been a lifelong ambition to cross the finish line with someone out there to greet me with open arms.

"Speaking of which, my last goal is to join Ann's family. After listening to her answer before, I do not think we'll have too much trouble accomplishing that goal. I am so looking forward a long and happy life for all of us. Her children are terrific and I want to be part of their lives—not to say that their dad has been at all neglectful of them. Actually, I find him a rather interesting man, a bit on the stodgy side, but a man of goodwill. If all goes as planned I would hope that Ann and I could marry within the year." (Ann is crying in earnest now that Mike has somehow managed to breach the barrier that has separated them for nearly a year.)

"I then gave Ann and Mike the next set of instructions the goal of which was to help them become more aware of their *self*-control *vs.* *other*-control:

Name two people you have "hired" to act in your life script whom you would now like to "fire" either because they do not handle their roles well or because they are uncooperative. How would the removal of these people influence your life? If you rid yourself of them, who will play their role (or did you decide that the role should be omitted from the play entirely)?

Assuming Control 91

Ann's responses:

"I hired Mike to be my partner and lover and that's working out better than I ever thought possible. A few of the people I allowed into my world, however, need to be exiled because the price I'm paying is too dear. One person is my girlfriend Kay. She's a wonderful woman, very talented and bright, but every time I see her I feel drained of energy. She experienced some personal crises a number of years ago and still hasn't resolved any of them. When we were younger she played the role of writing mentor, but now she just seems to want me to entertain her all the time. She doesn't work, she doesn't write, and she doesn't keep up her end of a conversation. I become annoyed with her and I feel tired after seeing her. This affects the amount of energy I have when I'm with Mike or with my children. I do not want to end our friendship but I do need to limit the time I spend with her. I do not think that at this point I need a mentor anymore, so I do not think I need to replace her.

"The other person is my agent, Doris. She's been with me for years. At first, everything seemed to be OK. Doris was attentive and worked hard to get my writing published. I did not mind paying her for her trouble. It was well worth it to be relieved of the burden of having to deal with the business end of things. Recently though, she has been preoccupied with other matters and with other clients. I understand that I'm not the only one in her stable of writers, but I do not think that means she can ignore my calls or my questions about her progress selling certain manuscripts. Before she became a successful agent she was more like a friend I could depend on. Now she's—well, like an agent who's always looking at the bottom line, that is, money. I resent it and I think that she no longer serves me well as my protector or my spokesperson. There are times when I get off the phone with her that I feel so angry that it takes me a couple of hours to compose myself. That's a price I'm not willing to pay. I'm giving her the boot as soon as I can terminate our contract, and that should be about 30 days after I send her written notification. I will need to replace her. I have the names of several agents recommended by friends. It will be a great relief to finally rid myself of someone who is obstructing my professional growth because of her selfishness."

Mike's responses:

"I can think of two people who play major roles in my life and whose roles I would change without a moment's hesitation. The first is a colleague at work. When we first met he was involved, ambitious, and a team player. Now that he has become successful, he has taken a path in another direction. Not that this is bad—not at all. But along the way, he seems to think nothing of manipulating his friends and colleagues, often with tragic consequences. It's got to the point

92   Couples at the Crossroad

where I look for ways to avoid him. If I could, I would just kick him out of my life completely. Unfortunately, he's now my supervisor and I can't simply fire him on the spot. He evaluates my work and reports directly to the president of the corporation. The good news is that when I finally transfer to the U.S., I'll be my own boss and I will report directly to the president. This is one case where I can remove a major player from my life script and not have to replace him.

"The other person who I need to be deal with is my brother, Micah. He's become completely self-absorbed. He and his wife haven't slept together for years. Their children essentially raised themselves and now do not seem to have one iota of the common sense they'll need if they are to survive in society. Micah has always been very thoughtful and kind. Now he is so preoccupied with his personal crises that he can't function—at home or at work. He won't open himself up to any one. He needs to rewrite his life script, and not include his wife in it. She's not a bad person, but the two are completely incompatible and it's torture to sit in the same room with them. The tension between them is thick enough to cut with a knife. I've tried to talk with Micah. I've offered to go to counseling. I've offered to take time off so we could take a long vacation and try to sort things out. He has refused every offer, and he refuses to recognize just how angry and depressed he is. I certainly do not want to terminate my relationship with him; he's too dear to me. But I do need to put some limits on the amount of time I spend with him, or I'll become as frustrated and depressed as he is. Again, fortunately, I'll be in the U.S. soon and I won't need to confront him directly about his behavior. Nonetheless, he is one of the actors in my life play that should spend less time on stage with me and more time with his children. I feel a bit guilty thinking these thoughts, but they are real, whether I feel guilty or not."

I then asked them to indicate how spending time with each of two people brought them closer to their goals, or how they diverted their attention from it.

Ann's response:

"When I'm not writing or spending time with my children or Mike, I spend a major portion of whatever free time I might have with two friends. One is my girlfriend, Carol, a fellow writer and a major source of support. The other person is my sister, Mary. I can't spend as much time as I would like with either of them, but the time I do spend with them is always valuable. My goals, as I mentioned before, include completing a new novel within the year. Carol has been enormously helpful in this area. She reads my work, makes intelligent critique, and offers ideas about changing thoughts, concepts, or words. I only spend about five hours a week with her. I wish I could triple it. Her insights help me enormously. She also seems to have an inexhaustible supply of professional manuals and books she is willing to loan me. And perhaps even more importantly, she urges me to go to conferences and to take courses. We go together; she supports me and I support her.

"Mary serves as the voice of reason. She calms me when I begin to lose perspective. She prods me along when I become too lazy. And she gives me hugs when I become discouraged. She really is a terrific person, and a wonderful sister. I only spend a few hours a week with her and that time is spent mostly on the phone. The time is absolutely invaluable to me. She keeps me headed in the right direction, whether that's writing or losing weight or thinking through the financial complexities of sending a child to college."

Mike's response:

"At this point, I do not spend a lot of time with anyone except Ann. I do not like being around my brother although we were very close when we were younger. I do not like spending time with my colleagues at work. I've never really had the need for a 'best friend' because I've always considered myself totally self-sufficient. Nowadays, I'm feeling a bit cheated that I do not have the kinds of relationships with other people that Ann has with Carol and Mary. It's my fault I know, but I do wish I could correct the situation. For example, maybe if I could hang around other runners I would be more optimistic about my plans to run the Boston marathon. I guess one of the problems that we've uncovered is exactly that—that no one influences me except me. It seems to be difficult for me to give up control, and I guess that brings us right back to where we started: intimacy and emotional closeness are very hard for me."

We have four alternatives when it comes to choosing the kind of relationship we want with certain people: (1) we can continue to associate with them as we did before; (2) we can restrict the time spent with them; (3) we can expand the number of hours we spend together; or (4) we can terminate the relationship with them completely.

Time spent with people in casual relationships is not time misspent, but it is important to recognize that major time spent on minor characters in our life script generally leads to minor results. As a rule of thumb, we should spend major time with major players and minor time with minor players.

9

Scripts Lovers Live

Soon after discussing mood chains with Mike and Ann, I ask them to describe the results of their first "fight." Ann recalled thinking, "Here we go again. Every time I think everything will turn out all right, something happens to mess things up."

Mike remembered how discouraged and disheartened he was. He also remembered how he was just as angry with his parents as he was with Ann. When I asked him why, he stated, "I remember wondering how I was going to make things better. Nobody had ever taught me that skill. When he and my mother fought, my father simply withdrew to the library and read. I guess I still use him as my model, although I know there's got to be a better way." Without knowing it, Ann and Mike were beginning to address the next topic: life scripts.

A quick assessment of the marital status of your friends will reveal that for some people something "always happens to mess things up" on a regular basis. The course of events leading up to the eventual breakup is almost entirely predictable. The only people surprised are the two people involved.

It's like a Greek tragedy: The audience knows exactly what to expect and tries to warn the "hero" or "heroine" who, because of some basic flaw in his or her otherwise noble character, fails to heed the warning. The fact is that most of us become involved in relationships that follow a specific course with a fully predictable outcome.

I told Ann and Mike that as a follow-up to our discussion about "toxic" personalities and mood chains, I wanted to delve more deeply into life scripts—scripts that virtually all people write for themselves at an early age. Life scripts reveal the basic decisions people make about their lives and about the paths they have chosen to follow.

Couples generally complement each other. The "bully" or domineering person either finds or elicits passivity in his or her partner. The do-gooder often elicits suspicion and distrust. As we look more deeply into these relationships, we find not only a reciprocation of attitudes, but also a long well-defined series of moves and countermoves that reflect the subconscious interpersonal games being played out.

Each of us plays a variety of roles in our interpersonal relationships. We agree, at least at an unconscious level, to obey certain well-established rules. Some of the life scripts we play out are relatively benign; others are destructive and may lead to emotional and/or physical harm to ourselves or to others.

Early Decisions

We, all of us, make decisions at a young age that (1) ensure human contact and stimulation, (2) provide structure and the comfort of routine, and (3) help us define an "existential position" consistent with our self-image and our self-esteem. Taken together, these elements make up a life script, a basic plan defining in concise terms where we want to go in our lives, and how we want to get there. It contains our earliest decisions about ourselves along with our prediction about what "should" happen in the future. Often our life scripts are clear to everyone but ourselves. Some scripts are "bad" because they lead to personal tragedy (alcoholism, depression, psychosis); some are "good" (being a leader, successful husband/wife, handsome prince/ss, effective parent, business wo/man); most fall somewhere in the middle.

A life script is a superficially simple declaration describing our role and intention in life. We *feel* the declaration—even if it is not *articulated*—in the first person singular. For example, a bad life script might be, "I am drinking myself to death," "I am working myself to death," or, less dramatically, "I am always trying to catch up." A "good" script might declare, "I am rescuing my family (nation)," or "I am bringing harmony to the world."

Whether a life script is benign or harmful depends on our earliest decisions about the nature of our relationship with others (including our relationship with the world, God, mother/father) and our relationship with ourselves. These relationships, boiled down to their very essence, represent four types of existential positions:

1. Type I: Happy, well-adjusted person. If I believe I'm OK and the world is OK, I will trust and feel accepted. If you (God, Mother/Father, my lover), tell me how smart I am or how pretty I am, I accept what you say, and I feel good about it. I feel happy and optimistic. I can grow up without the need for external support. I maintain well-defined boundaries that help me keep

96   Couples at the Crossroad

the hostile environment out—including abusive relationships, and help me tolerate uncomfortable feelings inside my skin boundary. I can adjust to adversity, and I can bounce back after failure.

2. Type II: Unhappy, Neurotic person. If I believe that I'm Not OK but you (the world, God, mother/father, my lover) are OK, I always feel a bit inferior, a bit stupid, or a bit ugly, no matter what you say. However, I want you to keep trying to convince me otherwise. I am unhappy but not totally miserable. I need support from the outside world, and I become "clingy" and dependent when I do not get it. My boundaries are loose, but I do maintain some control over what comes into my mind and my body, and what I intend to express emotionally and behaviorally. I am not very optimistic about life, and I have trouble adjusting when things get rough, but I manage to muddle through.

3. Type III: Narcissistic/Paranoid Person. I'm happy knowing I'm always right, and you are always wrong. It does not matter if you tell me nice things, because I will not believe you anyway. My job is to exploit you, manipulate you, and take advantage of every situation. If you feel unhappy about my behavior, I will pretend to care, but only until I can figure a way out of the problem. My boundaries are rigid. I will not let anybody know the real me. When my boundaries are breached, I will respond with irritability and possibly with violence. I do not really need you emotionally unless you are willing to confirm my superiority and support my grandiosity.

4. Type IV: Disorganized/Psychotic Person. I am not happy, and I know deep down you cannot be happy either because the world is falling apart. Nobody, including I myself, can be trusted. My boundaries are loose. My thoughts, feelings, and actions cannot be contained. The anger, violence, sadness, misery, malevolence, and disorganization around me permeate my boundaries so that I do not clearly understand what is happening to me. Sometimes, to make up for my anxiety and loss of control, I will hallucinate or make up myths (delusions) about my existence. I made up my mind about these things when I was very young—9 to 18 months old—so no one can tell me anything different. Sometimes, however, medication will help me keep my anxiety and my disorganization to a manageable level. I can then function fairly well in society.

Life Script Heroes

These early decisions serve as the bases for any script we choose to write. Depending on our existential position, we predict either a bad future or a relatively happy one. In either case, our early decisions remain with us in one form or another unless—this is the important point—we are able to recognize that our decisions were based on incomplete information, and that we may need to "re-decide" our position. The idea is to replace our malignant perception of the world with a less toxic one.

Once we have made our basic decisions about who we are and what we need, we need to find someone whose behaviors and attitudes serve as model for us. These models may come from fiction or from real life.

Most often, our parents serve this purpose. However, while our parents often demonstrate how we should play a particular role in our life scripts, they might not be able to show us how to play some of the more important ones. In this case, we choose, either consciously or unconsciously, someone else who can help us actualize our life plan. For example, a Type III (Narcissistic/Paranoid) person may be able to identify with his tyrannical father who teaches the "rules" for behaving in a superior and selfish fashion. However, a mythical character such as Captain Ahab, or a true to life character such as Hitler, provides a more dramatic and impressive model. From these characters, we not only learn the basic attitude of the Narcissist/Paranoid, but also the kinds of goals consistent with a Type III script.

A Type II person who believes she isn't very pretty or bright might well identify with a character in Cinderella or, if a male, model himself after the Beast in "Beauty and the Beast." These models define the beliefs and behaviors, which go along with a Type II script.

Whatever our early decisions may be, we need someone to emulate—someone who can teach us what we need to know to satisfy the demands of the life script we have written early in our lives. If our parents do not offer a good model, we will find someone else to do the job.

The Don'ts and the Do's

In addition to our early decisions about the meaning of life and a model to guide us, we are also influenced by the "voices" we have incorporated as part of our personality. Our life scripts are particularly affected by parental injunctions ("Do Not's") and parental attributions ("Do's"). While Dad's words might say, "Idle hands are the devil's handmaidens," his real demand is "Do not be playful" or "Do not be happy." When Mom says, "Big boys/girls do not cry," the message we get—and we believe—is "Do not feel." These kinds of messages reinforce our existential positions and force us to find someone, real or fictional, to show us how we can survive without happiness or without feelings. Is it any wonder that our children turn to gangs, the islands of power in a sea of misery and weakness?

It is easy to overlook the positive aspects of parental injunctions. After all, they do keep us from stealing and killing, and from coveting our neighbor's wife or husband. In this sense, they are essential for an orderly society. A man whose behavior has not been moderated on occasion can hardly be called civilized, let alone socialized. Nonetheless, unreasonable and unnatural demands produce stilted scripts and strained relationships with the significant people in our lives.

Equally damaging are "attributions"—the Do's—of social behavior. "Be brave," "Try harder," "Be a big boy/girl," "Always work hard," etc. are messages most of us received early and often. In themselves, they are good messages. However, when they are unreasonable, they become part of a tragic life script requiring a kind of perfectionism not entirely suited for ordinary humans.

To help us solve the problem of unrealistic attributions we turn again to our mythical heroes: Scarlet O'Hara, Captain Nemo, Superman, and Wonder Woman. Our heroes tell us how to deal with unreasonable but powerful demands, and we include their advice in our life scripts. For example, if the attribution is "Try harder," we might identify with Thomas Edison and become a workaholic; if the attribution is "Be smart," we might identify with Einstein and become a very serious student. We might be very satisfied with our role as a workaholic or serious student. However, when we couple with our lover and have children, our home life becomes something less than ideal. Our relationship, at all levels, becomes strained and all parties often become thoroughly miserable.

Men and women often share similar scripts. There are members of both sexes who represent happy, neurotic, narcissistic/paranoid, or disorganized/psychotic types. As many men as women have had the "Try harder" message drummed into them, just as there are as many women as men who have had to learn "Do not feel."

Lovers, of course, live many other kinds of scripts. Each is based on our early decisions about life, on our parents' injunctions and attributions, and on the people we choose as our models. It was clear from the beginning that Ann and Mike brought a catalogue of issues into the counseling room. We begin with Ann's story.

Ann's two previous husbands were similar: They were both highly touted professionals who worked long hours and subjugated their families to the demands of the job. And both were dependent on Ann for support and acknowledgment.

Her failed marriages seemed to be the direct result of early decisions. The decisions were based on the (unconscious) messages passed along to her by her mother who showed her "how" to reach certain goals, and inadvertently reinforced by her father who showed her "what" goals were worth achieving. Ann decided at the age of nine years she would prefer to be a good wife and mother rather than to be a professional. She was much too young to have made such a decision, but the decision matched the attitude of her mother and the other adult females with whom she had contact. She learned how to be a good mother from her mother, and Ann's father rewarded with his attention and adoration.

Ann's childhood was relatively happy; her parents demonstrated love, care, and thoughtfulness. However, they neglected to teach her the importance of anger. Without instruction in the proper use of anger, Ann became vulnerable to the whims and unreasonable demands of her spouses.

To help her cope with feelings of helplessness, Ann identified with TV actresses. She began to emulate the actress' attitudes and behavior. They became her mythical heroines, the people who could best help Ann develop a life script into which her values—the do's and do nots of life—could be incorporated. She was particularly drawn to the good/patient/spiritually enlightened types of women's roles.

As a result, Ann spent most of her time caring for her family. She was always prepared to set an extra place at the dinner table on five minutes notice. She drove her children to school, took her husbands' laundry to the cleaners, went to the Little League games, and, with the little energy left over, she prepared meals and kept the social calendar.

She often felt neglected and ignored. Deep down she hungered for the attention her husbands generally reserved for clients and friends. Her resentment grew, but it was never voiced; after all, she reasoned, this was what being a good mother and wife was all about.

She was unhappy and she was lonely. She wanted others to acknowledge her as something more than a servant. The unhappiness took its toll. Ann's inability to express her anger directly and effectively ultimately drained her of joy and spontaneity. When her husbands wanted to enjoy physical closeness, Ann became "frigid," a covert attempt to punish them for their lack of attention and warmth. In moments of despair, she wondered why her family did not respect her; after all, she was always so "nice," "sacrificed everything for her family," and "never got angry."

She began to feel used and cheated, and she had seriously entertained the idea of suicide, all the while chauffeuring the kids from game to game and setting an extra place at mealtime for her husbands' cronies.

Ann's script required her to sacrifice herself and her needs for others. It was based on the early teachings of her parents and on her attempt to emulate a mythical heroine. It was not successful because every time she worked out a formula for happiness, she did not include herself in the equation. The resulting disappointment and bitterness nearly drove her mad. She was strong enough, however, to end two destructive relationships and to regain her sense of dignity and pride through a painful process of psychotherapy and a commitment to change.

As we worked together, a picture of the couple's needs and desires emerged. Mike, of course, had developed his own life script as a youngster. At the age of fourteen, he had put all the pieces together and decided academic achievement and the pursuit of intellectual matters were priorities in his life. His father had also been an "intellectual" who emphasized the usefulness of the rational mind. He let Mike know through his attitudes and behavior that he discounted feelings, his father observing that emotions produced discomfort in some cases, and a complete loss of control in others.

Mike learned his lessons well. He always "used his head"—as his mother was fond of telling her friends. His heroes included Albert Einstein and Bertrand Russell; however, he was never able to emulate their ability to balance intellect with emotion. His favorite book was Twenty Thousand Leagues Under the Sea, and when he wasn't busy "using his head," he was thinking about improbable but heady futuristic thoughts. Ultimately, Mike became emotionally detached, but financially successful. He became a corporate lawyer, earning more money in a single year than his father had earned in a lifetime.

Unfortunately, the emphasis on rational thought and logic had robbed him of the opportunity to experience love and warmth. He felt empty and incomplete as a man. His only marriage failed largely as a result of his choosing as a bride a woman even more rational and more detached than he was. The two spent many hours planning the relationship and figuring out how best to meet their financial and social needs. Somehow, it never worked out. Neither could satisfy the submerged but powerful need for intimacy and closeness. After several years of frustration, they parted amiably, noting that the "spark" simply was not there.

As Mike grew up, he began to feel "ugly inside." He had always sensed there was something "missing" in his life. However, the vocabulary of the rational view did not include concepts such as warmth, self-sacrifice, and compassion, and therefore he could not identify the problem. His early decisions about life had not allowed him to accept the kindness of others, or, perhaps more importantly, to fully trust what others told him.

With the death of his father, the support for Mike's script weakened. Mike began to reread Einstein and Russell. He began to question why his marriage failed. He was able to better understand that, unless he could balance his intellect with compassion and spontaneity, there could be little happiness in a relationship. This insight prompted him to consider the possibility of an alternative approach to life. The result of this decision was a spiritual pilgrimage, which took him to Tibet, the Ashrams of Colorado and the Encounter Groups of Esalen at Big Sur in California. He had been home merely two weeks when he heard about the convention Ann was to attend and decided it was time to try out some of the new thinking he'd picked up along the way.

Mike had developed a script requiring him to be logical and rational, to "use his head." Intelligence and education were valued above all else by his parents. He followed the tenets laid down by his father's religious fervor for intellectuality. Had Mike's father remained alive to reinforce his earlier teachings, it is doubtful that Mike would have had the incentive to make badly needed changes. He would have continued to "plan" good relationships, instead of balancing his successful career with the joy of spontaneity and creativity. Ann's affection gave him an opportunity to express his caring and, more importantly, to use his rational mind for altruistic purposes. It gave him an opportunity, in short, to change a possibly tragic script into a more benevolent one.

Life Script Exercises

To help Ann and Mike understand the importance of life scripts, I asked them to go back to the earliest memories they had of their parents, caretakers, or other powerful adults in their lives. The "best" memories, for the purposes of this exercise, were the ones representing events occurring prior to the age of four. After each had sifted through half dozen memories or so, I asked each to summarize in his mind what he believed to be his essential belief about himself and about the world. For example, let's say that the earliest memories included: (1) being punished for getting dirty, (2) witnessing the behavior of an alcoholic parent, (3) being embarrassed by a nursery school teacher, and (4) not being able to run as

102   Couples at the Crossroad

quickly as other children. The cumulative impact of these memories might have led to the belief, "I'm small and weak; everyone is stronger, smarter, and prettier than I am." I told Ann and Mike, "Describe your early decision about yourself, your relationship with the world, and your "existential position.""

Ann's response: "I remember being carried home by my mother from a friend's house. It was very late and I was tired. She was tired too, but she picked me up and carried me, and I'll never forget how that made me feel."

My response: "How did it make you feel?"

Ann's response: "It made me feel small but protected. It also made me feel spoiled, like maybe I would never have to worry about anybody not being there if I really needed them." (Ann became sad, and her eyes moistened for a moment.)

"Do you see any relationship between that decision and your relationship with men?"

Ann's response: "Unfortunately, it's all too clear. I always expect to be 'cared for' and I always find someone who is strong enough to 'carry' me both financially and emotionally. I wonder if I'll ever outgrow that feeling. I'm like one of those Type II neurotics who seem to be so dependent on everyone. Come to think of it, even though she worked hard, I always felt close to that maid in the movie, *Gone with the Wind*. My script seems to be 'Depending on you.'"

Ann began to cry in earnest at that point. Mike put his arm around her shoulder and gave her the hug she seemed to need.

It was Mike's turn. I said, "Have you been able to come up with an early memory that summarizes your view of the world?"

Mike seemed to be reluctant to speak. I urged him on.

"I remember a time when I drowned four little kittens."

Ann and I both looked at him. Mike looked down, ashamed, saddened, perhaps even terrified by his admission. I did not need to say anything.

"I must have been three or four years old. Our cat had delivered a litter of beautiful kittens in the closet in our living room. It had happened before—unwanted kittens—and the solution to the problem seemed to be to get rid of them by placing them in a paper bag and simply throwing them into the river. It was common practice where we lived. The older children in the neighborhood seemed to think nothing of it. I had no idea of the meaning or the value of life or death. I thought that was simply the way it's done. I wanted to be like everyone else, so I threw the poor kittens into the river, thinking perhaps that somehow they would float down to a field or somewhere where they would be safe. I wonder now if my position on abortion has something to do with that simple gesture—the murder of four little kittens."

The confession was overwhelming. Mike had rediscovered a memory that he had long ago buried—a memory that revealed his need to be accepted by everyone else.

Mike continued: "With regard to my existential position—that's a hard one. I had thought that I was one of your Type I "Happy" people. Now I'm not so sure. Maybe I'm just a Type II neurotic who needs a lot of loving. My script is 'Following orders' or maybe 'Needing to be accepted.'" Another admission, another step forwards.

We then discussed models who served to help implement the early script decisions. Ann's model turned out to be comedienne, Gracie Allen, a supposed ditzy woman fully dependent on her husband, comedian George Burns, and extremely funny. "I always liked Gracie Allen," Ann said, "because she was able to be dependent without being self-conscious or embarrassed by it."

Mike's model was his father, who, despite his emotional coolness, was able to show Mike how to be aloof and yet who somehow managed to get the attention he needed from his wife and co-workers. His mother had taught him that in order to be socially and professionally accepted Mike had to learn how to be charming. His father taught him that humor and intelligence were the two ways to accomplish these goals, although he—Mike's father—seemed to have relatively little of the former and an overabundance of the latter.

We next talked about attributions and injunctions. Ann recalled that her mother always emphasized the virtue of self-sacrifice and the need to "hold your tongue" no matter how angry you were. The reason was, she told Ann, that patience and the suppression of anger were not only signs of maturity, but also signs of "class," an attribute that "makes all the difference in the world" when it came time to attract the "right kind of man."

Mike's parents emphasized the need to "be logical" and to be "responsible." His father was fond of saying, "Do not be silly" despite the fact that, after a few drinks, he could become uproariously whimsical, witty, and just plain silly himself. The result was Mike's very serious and business-like appreciation of humor. Fortunately, Ann was able to reduce the seriousness and increase the humor in a more balanced way.

Both Ann and Mike agreed that the only cure for them was to be together forever. Who was I to argue?

Stage III
Secret Fears, Secret Desires

10

Hidden Realities

Falling in love (connecting) and being in love (coupling) are different. The difference lies in the impact of time and experience. While the quality and intensity of the relationship may not differ, there is nonetheless a ripening, a maturing of the process of being together. Subtle changes appear in the way we interact with, and in the way we perceive the person who has finally made it through the layers of our doubts, and the filters of our desires.

Stage III offers another choice point for people who think they are in love. While the relationship has passed a series of tests, most often it has not yet been galvanized by the passage of time. During the initial stage of coupling, decisions were simple. We studied our lover's behavior, got a sense of where he's coming from emotionally, calculated the impact of his history and the medical/social/financial pressures on him, and determined whether we can tolerate his personal life style. With time, we were better able to gauge the more subtle aspects of compatibility: moods, scripts, and emotional comfort levels.

By the time we reach the third stage of coupling, we have established a satisfactory comfort level. We have learned to trust our lover with our feelings and with our vulnerabilities. We have developed a deep concern and compassion for him. We want to protect him or her from hurt and unhappiness. Nonetheless, most of us harbor hidden feelings—desires and fears—that influence our relationship. We are determined to please (and to be pleased by) our partner, but the task can be daunting unless we can expose and confront the hidden realities that govern so much of our behavior.

Courage

Ann and Mike had already been able to test the viability of their relationship. Despite their concerns about Mike's readiness for commitment, they decided to keep plugging along because, while neither one was "ideal," each offered the

108 Couples at the Crossroad

other enough passion, intimacy and commitment to evoke good feelings about himself and about the world. Had they decided that there was no realistic chance of resolving differences in lifestyle, values, motivation, emotional climates, or in life scripts, they simply would have removed themselves from the situation. However, they had invested months in the relationship, and breaking up at this point would have been heart-rending.

The process of parting is more difficult than the process of coupling. During the process of coupling, the contact and connection phases often are based on differences, and differences produce excitement. Excitement reinforces romantic notions. As a relationship develops, couples work hard to find points of agreement and to develop a sense of togetherness. Each person learns to adapt to his lover's view of the world, and to accept his flaws and eccentricities. In short, each member of the couple learns to balance the seesaw, balancing the differences with the sameness' that lead to stability and to security.

Quitting a relationship during Stage III is the emotional equivalent of investing our paycheck in a business going bankrupt: The "creditors" we hear pounding at the door are the nagging doubts, the dreams and the fantasies about what could have been "if only...."

To quit now, we would have to physically remove ourselves from our lover, an arduous task after so many months—perhaps years—of emotional investment. We would also have to retool our emotions for yet another sortie into yet another contact-connection-coupling Tilt-A-Whirl with yet another candidate for our affections.

Splitting up requires stamina and a not-easily-described quality of character called "courage." Courage is the most important of all the tools for changing various aspects of our lives. Without it, we cannot make changes; with it, we can make almost any change we want to make.

Courage in relationships transcends logic and reason; it comes from a process much more profound than simply "figuring things out." It comes from the ultimate "moment of truth," the precise moment when, upon laying our head on the pillow before a fitful sleep, we are able to clearly say, "This isn't going to work," and to then take action, recognizing we are about to enter an emotional marathon requiring time, patience, and resilience.

Moments of Truth

The completion of the exercises at the end of the previous sections gave Ann and Mike some "truths" about their courtship. They had already decided about the viability of their coupling. Nonetheless, a vague sense of indecision prevailed. Each of them had secret thoughts and feelings that centered on their largely unconscious resentments and disappointments. Direct confrontation of these feelings was the only way for them to make their final decision about a lifetime commitment to each other.

Certain exercises were developed to clarify the nature of their discontent. They magnified strengths and weaknesses, and they helped Ann and Mike better appreciate why their relationship was so important to them. Crucial to the success of completing the exercises was an understanding and an appreciation of the concept of change and the whole notion of awareness.

The Paradox of Change

The paradoxical secret of changing ourselves often is to do nothing, but rather to become "aware." Deliberate attempts to change will frequently fail. Our mind and our emotions resist change the same way the infant resists an unpalatable dose of strained spinach.

The resistance is expressed through the voice of the recalcitrant child in all of us—the part of us that says, "You can't push me around!" in response to a critical parent voice that demands that we "do better" next time.

With the resistance come fragmented feelings and thoughts. Part of us wants to change, the child's voice saying, "I need to change because mother/father will abandon us if I do not." But there is another part—just as strong—that doesn't want to change. This voice declares, "I'm an adult and I do not need you to tell me what to do!"

The battle between these two parts leaves us exhausted and drained, and the coercive attempt to change results in conflict, confusion, and uncertainty. These feelings make our efforts to change hardly worth the time and the effort. At best, our changes will be temporary. At worst, we impede, distort, and disguise our real needs and, along with them, the true nature of our relationship with our lover.

The question is, "If we can't deliberately change ourselves or our situation, how will change occur?" The answer is: awareness of who we are, and what we need to do to sustain authenticity—an honest appreciation of our needs and our desires.

Changes in our awareness lead automatically to other changes in our lives. For example, to develop self-esteem and a more benevolent self-image, we need to increase an awareness of our skills, our talents, and our essential goodness. To

110   Couples at the Crossroad

develop a joy of life and spontaneity, we need to increase our awareness of the *now* moment, and we need to learn to let go of the past.

The trick is to appreciate our own experience of the world, to let ourselves flow with our feelings and thoughts, without resisting momentary discomfort. Change born of awareness brings with it an intuitive recognition of what is healthy and alive for us in the present, in the now.

The Nature of Awareness

We cannot easily understand awareness in the abstract because as soon as we become aware of an experience, we lose it. Awareness refers to a life *process* that cannot be divided into its parts. It is an ever-changing experience of how we (inside the skin boundary) respond to the world around us (outside the skin boundary), and how we bridge the two worlds through picture-thoughts. The awareness of our internal world and our external world constantly changes; we can never experience it exactly the same way twice. Just as we cannot take a handful of river water and say, "This is the river," we cannot take a handful of awareness—take a Polaroid picture of an ongoing experience—and say, "this is reality."

Awareness requires perceiving ourselves within the context of our life space. Our life space includes all the elements influencing our behavior at any given time. These may include personal influences, environmental influences, or the more elusive influences of politics, economics, and institutions (media, education, societal decrees, religion, or philosophy).

Becoming aware means the simultaneous perception of three states of being: (1) our internal sensations and feelings, (2) our experiences of external or "real" things, and (3) our world of picture-thoughts. It is a full time job. People who want to succeed in their relationships want to know about themselves, and about the world out there. They want to know how much they can grow spiritually and emotionally; they want to expand their boundaries to include the *not-me* experiences. They want to enjoy a good laugh, and to experience being alive *right here* and *right now*. Moreover, they want most of all to contribute to the beauty and dignity of their lover.

We can recognize truly aware people easily: They are spontaneous, curious, competent, perceptive, sensitive, optimistic, cooperative, and sharing. They move around with a certain grace and aplomb. Their boundaries are loose enough to welcome us in, and yet strong enough to resist annoying or harmful intrusions from external pressures. They are aware of their environment—internal and external—in ways that most of us will never experience.

Hidden Realities   111

Awareness is critical to compatibility with our lover, compatibility with our own needs, fears and desires, and compatibility with our ever-evolving life circumstances. This compatibility mirrors our appreciation of the three spheres of awareness.

There are three spheres of awareness. The first is an awareness of the outside world. This refers to our ability to make full contact with everything on the other side of the contact boundary. These include things like smells, tastes, sounds, tangibles, and sights—everything we experience out there at the present moment.

It is made up of people, places, jobs, family, hobbies, the highest mountains, the reddest sunsets, the bluest skies, and the whitest snows. It also contains the best books and the most delicious meals. In short, it is the place where we make contact with the experiences that move us to tears, laughter, and anger, where we earn our wages, and where we strain our muscles. And it is the place where we exchange our potential for the good life for the reality of joy.

Stimulation from the outer world is so important that, fully deprived of it for even a few hours, we become "psychotic" in the sense that we begin to hallucinate in an attempt to fill the void. For example, there has been recent research indicating that over 60% of the spouses who survive the death of their mates after long marriages experience auditory and/or visual hallucinations connected with their deceased partners.

If we cannot directly experience the other side of what each of us calls *me*, we will simulate the environment through fantasies so powerful that they may become our reality. In short, we must establish outer world stimulation, if we are to maintain a palatable life. Is it any wonder adults locked in solitary confinement or emotionally withdrawn children behave in such odd ways?

Bones, skin, muscles, and tissues make up our bodies. They represent both the foundation and the protective shelter for our physical being. They also represent the seat of our sensations and emotions, the domains dominating the world on *this* side of our skin-boundary. The integrity of bodily functions depends on our diligence in repairing the body when it breaks down, and on reinforcing its strength with food, vitamins, and exercise. Excesses of any kind serve to destroy the body's integrity as surely as wind, rain, and corrosion conspire to weaken our strongest homes and buildings. Lungs filled with smoke, brain cells battered by alcohol, muscles compromised by junk foods, and hearts hardened by cholesterol often leave in their wake tragic illness and death.

The unprotected and weakened body is vulnerable to physical dis-ease and to emotional dis-ease as well. Bad thoughts and bad feelings, grouchiness and irritability, depression, and cynicism are signs that we have begun to take our bodies

112   Couples at the Crossroad

for granted. Unlike old cars, we can't trade in our physical selves every two years no matter how dysfunctional they become.

In the inner world—the world on *this* side of the contact boundary—we experience sharp contacts with sensations such as itching, tension, and warmth, and with feelings such as anger, happiness, contentment, and sadness. We own these experiences; we understand them to belong to us, and we take full responsibility for them.

Outer world and inner world awareness have one thing in common: reality. Itching and palpitations of the heart are as real as the smell of a rose or the feel of silk. While the inner world is subjective—a world no one else can experience—the outer world is objective and verifiable. The two worlds taken together make up what most people call real world.

The third zone occupies the smallest space, but also contains the greatest potential for comfort and personal success. This is the place where imagination and thinking replace sensing and experiencing. It is our mental and spiritual zone. It reflects precisely how our bodies and the environment meet, and how we negotiate the process of living. The interaction between the body and the environment creates the thing we call mind, the exact whereabouts of which is unknown, and will always be unknown. Some people would suggest that in actuality it is an internalized image of our godliness or our soul. I wouldn't disagree.

This third sphere of awareness is especially important when we talk about relationships, because it comprises fantasies that have no verifiable basis in reality. Fantasy includes experiences like imagination, thinking, planning, guessing, stage fright, and memories. The experiences can't be measured per se; however, we can measure the effect our fantasies have on our behavior. Tightened jaws, knotted stomachs, panic attacks, feelings of betrayal, "paranoid" thoughts, and infatuation are just several of the many ways we know that fantasy is exerting its influence on us and, inevitably, on our relationships.

While the process of fantasizing takes place in the present, the content of fantasy is timeless. Our imaginings, thoughts, and planning pay no heed to reality. We are restricted by neither inner strivings nor outer pressures; our fantasies take on a life of their own without regard to bodily sensations or societal demands. We can fantasize about the past or the future; we can hallucinate the smell of the rose, or a frightening tactile sensation of bugs crawling over our bodies. Whatever the content of our fantasies, we do not make full contact with the inner/outer world experience, and we, therefore, have abandoned a sacred event at the contact boundary.

Hidden Realities   113

Fantasy is extremely important to us. Within each imagining, within each picture, there is a truth—a germ of some hidden reality that teaches us something about ourselves, and about our immediate relationship with our lover. With these thoughts, Ann and Mike were about to enter the world of fantasy, a world that would reveal hidden needs and desires.

In order to prepare Ann and Mike for several intense experiences designed to help them ferret out the hidden truths behind their relationship, I asked them first to allow themselves to contact all three spheres of awareness—the outer world, the inner, and the fantasy world. I cautioned them not to be disappointed if they became confused, uncomfortable, anxious, or self-conscious. Each exercise, I told them, would bring a certain kind of awareness that would help them understand the essence of their relationship. I told them that truth was the end objective; effective communication was the means.

Both admitted they had difficulty expressing maximum truth with a minimum of discomfort. I reminded them that growth took time, that they not be impatient, and above all that they studiously avoid deliberately changing either themselves or each other.

11

Exercises in Awareness

The sophisticated reader will want to examine the following material very carefully. The exercises take time, but the results are guaranteed to startle you and perhaps with luck also to enlighten you. While they appear to be simple, these small personal experiments have proven to be extraordinarily difficult for most people. Since the first exercise formed the foundation for all future exercises, I suggested that Ann and Mike spend as much time as they needed to complete it.

Exercise 1: The Three Spheres

I asked Ann and mike to do the following exercise:

Sit in a comfortable position. Become aware of all three zones. Become aware of one inner world experience (for example, heartbeat, breathing, sensations). Then become aware of one outer world experience (for example, the warmth of the room, feet touching the floor), and then one fantasy world experience (for example, wondering whether you are doing the exercise correctly, or planning for the dinner party Saturday night). Become an observer of your awareness. Tell yourself what your awareness is: "Here and now I am aware of (tension in my neck, music on the stereo, imagining what my lover is doing, etc.). Repeat the cycle five times; that is, five internal awareness', five external awareness', and five fantasy awareness', always in the same order. Notice where your awareness wanders. Do you feel more comfortable becoming aware of inner or with outer world experiences? Are you able to follow a fantasy to its "logical" conclusion, or is your train of thought disrupted by competing fantasies?

Appreciate the difference between fantasy and reality. Notice that when you focus on fantasy, inner/outer experiences disappear and vice versa. Notice how you describe your experiences. Do you use verbs (e.g., the picture makes me happy), sensations (e.g., my arm is tensing up) or feeling words (e.g., this exercise makes me nervous)? Do you find yourself remembering events from the past, or perhaps wondering about things in the future? Stay with the process of experiencing your world. How long can you concentrate before you are distracted by a thought or a picture?

After you have trained yourself to become aware of the three zones, conjure up a picture of your lover. Follow the image of your lover as it changes. (Remember when you were a kid and you watched clouds form and reform into various shapes or images?) Become aware of the effect your lover's image/actions have on you. Do you begin to experience tension, excitement, or anger? Do you perhaps begin to want to fantasize about what s/he is doing at this moment, or about what will happen in the future? Get in touch with the quality of the experiences. What is the message—the truth—behind the pictures? Use an "I" statement to summarize the message: for example, "I get so mad when I think about how s/he treats me" or "I really miss him/her."

Ann's response:

"I had a hard time with this exercise. What I was experiencing outside kept getting mixed up with what I was experiencing on the inside. I tried taking turns, going from one zone to another and it did not work. I became totally confused and exhausted. My thoughts were so strong, I couldn't get in touch with the outside sounds or the sensation of touch. No matter how hard I tried, the thoughts kept coming. Not that they were bad thoughts. It was just that they wouldn't stop. Thoughts and pictures got jumbled up and it was as if they forced me to pay attention to them even though I did not want to. Then, when I was really upset with myself, I could actually feel Mike's arms around me and the thoughts disappeared and all I had was this beautiful feeling of not being alone and being safe. The message I got was "I do not want to be without you."

Ann looked at Mike. He looked down to the floor for a brief minute, before gazing at her and smiling. I intervened at that point, asking him what he experienced during the awareness exercise.

"Actually, I was able to go from one sphere to another without difficulty. I could hear my heart beating, then heard the air conditioner, then imagined Ann and I were walking on the beach at Plum Island. I went through the routine several times until finally, like Ann, I became confused. I found myself resorting to my senses whenever the confusion came over me—hearing the sounds outside or touching the sofa or maybe smelling the coffee. Suddenly a picture sprouted up inside my head. There was a woman far away. At first I thought it was my mother, but as the woman walked slowly toward me, I could see clearly that it was Ann, looking beautiful and very sexy. She came to me, arms open, eyes looking right through me, just as she's looking at me right now. It was at that point that I lost contact with all other sensations, thoughts, in fact, all other awareness. The message was clear to me: 'I can't live without this woman.'"

Exercise 2: Becoming You Becoming Me

I asked Ann and Mike to let their attention wander until something "grabbed" it. Precisely thirty seconds later, I told them:

Focus on the object. Appreciate its structure: is it round, square or a combination of shapes? Is it heavy, light, or weightless? Imagine what it would be like if you were the object. What would you experience? For example: if your attention rests on a lamp, what would you experience if you were a lamp? ("I am a lamp. I am bright. I am useful because I enable others to see when it's dark outside, etc.") After you identify with the object for several minutes, discover what you and the object really have in common. Perhaps you really are bright, and you really do enlighten people with your wisdom or intelligence. What truth can you learn about yourself that you may have forgotten or never truly appreciated before? Spend about five minutes on this exercise. If you have difficulty with it the first time, try it again.

Once you have gleaned a truth about yourself, imagine that you tell your lover about it. What is his/her reaction to it? Does s/he appreciate your skills, talents, or potential?

Ann's response:

"OK. When you told us to focus, I was looking at the sofa. I *am* the sofa. I am comfortable and inviting. I am soft and durable. You can spill things on me, sit on me for years, make love on me, doing whatever you want and I will still endure. I am solid and strong. You can depend on me. Do you hear me, Mike? You can depend on me." Then turning her head toward me, she announced that inside her head, when she told Mike he could depend on her, he told her, "Yes I know…I've always known."

Mike's response:

"I am a bookcase. I protect the world's greatest literature. I make room for diversity in size and talent. I am strong, well built, sturdy. I only need a minimum of polish and I look gorgeous. I invite you to look through my books, to find the beauty of words, and to enter the world of great thoughts."

Ann responded quickly. "And I will accept your invitation."

Exercises in Awareness   117

Exercise 3: Contact/Withdrawal

When they were ready, I asked Ann and Mike to engage in a series of personal experiments constructed to test the underpinnings of their relationship. It was important for them to learn how to confront each other directly about their experiences and to discuss their feelings truthfully. The results led to the first shreds of discord, but it was short-lived—much to the relief of both people. I told them:

By now, you realize that the contact boundary marks the place where the environment and the thing called 'I' meet. It's the place where we accommodate the world around us. There would be no laughter, no breathing, no creativity without contact with the environment. There are times, however, when withdrawal from the environment serves a very good purpose. The following exercise offers an opportunity to learn more about the contact/withdrawal process.

Begin by experiencing as completely as possible your external world. How do you experience the temperature in the room, the chair you're sitting on, the clothes you are wearing, the sounds surrounding you, etc. Are they pleasant, unpleasant, or neutral?

When you have a sense of the external world, close your eyes and let yourself withdraw. Give yourself permission to let your mind wander anywhere it would like to go.

Experience what it is like to deliberately leave your environment. Where does your imagination lead you? To a place inside the skin-boundary? Outside? Is it more exciting, more rejuvenating, more relaxing, more colorful, more populated, or perhaps less comfortable?

Now come back to the here and now of your environment. How do you experience the transition? Would you rather be in the outer zone of your environment or in the fantasyland you just left?

Now close your eyes once again and allow your mind to wander. Do you go back to the same place as before? Open your eyes and compare the experiences. What is it like in here compared to out there?

Ann responded first. "I like being 'out there.' I think that's why I became a writer in the first place. I could go anywhere and do anything I wanted to do. I could be with anyone I wanted to be with, and if I did not like something I could change it. I become energized when I'm in my fantasy world, and while I realize I need come back to reality every once in a while, I find most daily chores pure drudgery."

Mike admitted to occasional lapses in his preference for more realistic activities, but generally he enjoyed the competitive world. "My energy," he said,

118   Couples at the Crossroad

"comes not from battling fictions and monsters. I enjoy the competition of real people in real time."

"How does this affect your relationship with Ann," I asked.

"Why, it makes it sexier and more exciting!"

"Sexier and more exciting?" I was confused.

"Why of course! Ann's wonderful imagination and her fantasy world completely complement my need for real time structure. She imagines it, and I make it happen! It works out perfectly. She fantasizes and writes about it; I read it and bring it to reality."

I only needed to look at Ann's smiling face to know that the two really had learned how to make their differences work for them.

Withdrawal into fantasy serves us best when it allows us to escape difficult or painful realities. Under extreme stress, we can withdraw back to a time and a place when we felt better and behaved better. With luck, when we return to the real more difficult situation, we can bring back with us the excitement and the power that we find in the withdrawn state. The additional energy we find in our fantasyland helps us cope with a less-than-comfortable reality.

Clearly, too much withdrawal leads to isolation, a state of mind that, by its very nature, precludes the kind of human contact necessary to relieve loneliness. It is likewise clear that prolonged withdrawal from very difficult situations will only exacerbate the difficulties.

The solution to the dilemma is to make contact with the unpleasant, disturbing reality until we feel marginally uncomfortable, and then to withdraw into our inner world until we can rejuvenate ourselves, and then to return and prepare ourselves for the next skirmish with adversity.

All three zones of awareness are useful and necessary, but preoccupation with any specific zone brings a host of problems. For example, too much fantasy activity, because it disrupts full contact with the real world, may prevent us from dealing effectively with everyday issues. The lack of balance produces a loss of awareness, and diminishes our ability to function optimally.

When we feel threatened, our hearts beat faster; our blood pressure increases and our muscles tense up to prepare us for battle or for retreat. If, however, we only imagine a threat, our rapid heart rate and the accompanying preparations for fight or flights sap us of our energy, and we find that even the simplest tasks become burdensome. Another example: if we have "stage fright" and imagine others will judge our performance harshly, we experience the discomfort of "self-consciousness." Our fantasy has generated a catastrophic expectation, and makes us want to remove ourselves from the threatening situation. Here we are, center

Exercises in Awareness 119

stage: we want to run, and yet we are compelled to remain. The result is a battle between the part of us that wants to withdraw (to inhibit behavior) and the part that wants to run (to exhibit behavior). With so much energy devoted to keeping control, there is little energy left over to do our act (asking for a date, making a toast, making a speech, etc.).

On the other hand, too little involvement in fantasy will also drain us of our energy. A constant barrage of immutable stress—poverty, illness, loss of a lover, arguments at home—may lead to a variety of physical and emotional illness as well as just plain misery. Fantasy provides us with a reservoir of hope and excitement. The irony is that too much fantasy leads to conflict, confusion, and disintegration; too much harsh reality leads to the same set of disruptive behaviors!

As the last step in this exercise, I asked Ann and Mike to remember their most recent intimate contact. I suggested that they get a sense of what it was like to be with each other in a particular setting, doing a particular thing. I then suggested that they withdraw into their by-this-time familiar fantasyland, bringing their images of intimacy with them. I asked them to compare the two experiences. Was the remembered real situation more satisfying and comfortable? Or, rather, did the fantasy feel more secure and exciting? Ann and Mike each completed this sentence:

Compared to my real lover, my fantasy lover is _____?

Ann's response: "Compared to my real lover, my fantasized lover is tame and somewhat inept!"

Mike's response: "Compared to my real lover, my fantasy lover could learn a few things!"

Ann and Mike enjoyed each other in real life, and, while they readily admitted to having wonderful imaginings about each other, nothing could compare to their being with one another in an embrace of intimacy. I was beginning to wonder why they had sought counseling in the first place.

Exercise 4: Create-A-Product

The "Create-A-Product" exercise is a good tool for learning about self-image and self-esteem, important determinants of the success or failure in any relationship. Self-image comprises the totality of pictures, thoughts, and feelings we have about ourselves. How we see ourselves today will establish to a very large degree how we will behave, think, and feel tomorrow.

I asked Ann and Mike to begin the exercise with this simple task:

120   Couples at the Crossroad

Think of a product you feel society needs or values. The product can be anything. Be creative. Let your mind be silly or serious. For example, golfers may be interested in an automatic ball chaser. A psychotherapist may be interested in inventing an inflatable grandmother who tells children how good they are. Or perhaps you could come up with a disposable car because it is affordable and easy to get rid of when you are bored with it.

After you have thought of a product, think up a slogan for marketing it (for example, "Fly the Friendly Skies," "Progress is Our Most Important Product," etc.). Then think of a way to advertise it. Write the copy you would use to describe it in a magazine or on a T.V. commercial; imagine what pictures you would use to get your message across.

In your head, try to "sell" the product to your lover. Does he want to buy it? Does he think it is valuable, too silly, too expensive, too superficial, etc.?

If you were your lover, would you consider buying it? If not, why not? If you were to consider buying it, of what value would it be to you?

Here is the most difficult part of the exercise. Remembering how you proceeded in Experiment # 2, become the product you created. Describe yourself, pointing out the features, advantages and benefits. Example: 'I am a disposable automobile. I am small and good looking. I give you good service for a period of one year, and then you can throw me away. I'll never become boring to you, and I'll never cost more than you can afford.'

Now, pretend you <u>are</u> your lover. Truthfully respond as to whether the product is worth buying. Example: 'I (as your lover) will not buy you because I'm looking for a classy automobile that will last a lifetime. At times, I might become bored, but it is worth a little boredom to have a reliable automobile.

Although I generally reserve this particular exercise for group workshops, it can be an extremely powerful tool when used properly with couples "at the crossroad." I handed Ann and Mike each a sheet of paper to record their responses and, after precisely six minutes (two minutes for each task), I asked them to sit comfortably facing each other. Their job, I suggested, was to share the results as truthfully as possible.

Ann's response: "My product is a new kind of rifle that shoots 'relaxation' rays that won't hurt anybody, but would make them sit down and talk instead. The slogan would be something like, 'Kill 'em with kindness.' The product would be advertised in all men's magazines. The copy would say something like, 'Kill your enemy with kindness and never be angry or frightened again.'"

Exercises in Awareness 121

Mike's response: "I took a different approach to the exercise. My product was more practical, I guess. My product is an anti-virus program that works on people rather than computers. You plug someone in and within minutes you know where the problems are, and the program repairs the fault automatically. Not only that, but it also builds a firewall against other possible hazards to your health. The slogan would be something like 'Make proper reparations perfectly. Buy HIAV—The Human Immuno Anti Virus.' I would advertise the product in medical magazines, health-related magazines, and in major news magazines."

I suggested that Ann become her product and "sell" herself to Mike. Apparently sensing it that it was going to be a difficult job, she took and deep breath and said, "I'm reliable and last for ever. You can use me to make friends out of enemies. No more killing, no more harm. Use me and I'll faithfully protect you and your family."

The next part of the experiment was more difficult. I asked Mike to sit face to face with Ann and to let her know honestly whether she was worth "buying."

"Ann," he began, "I know you are the most reliable person in the world, but I can't buy you."

Ann was dumbstruck. I could see her shrivel up inside.

"Let me tell you why I can't buy you," Mike continued. "Killing 'em with kindness just doesn't work in the real world. Turning the other cheek is hardly the approach any man worth his salt would use if his family were in trouble."

It looked like Mike might have bought some trouble with his comments. I was eager to see what he would say next and how Ann would respond.

When it was his turn to share his product with Ann, Mike said, "I am an Anti-Virus that will protect you from health problems and repair you if an illness slips by. I last forever. Just plug me in and I will safeguard you."

Ann had pulled herself together by the time he had finished his statement. "I shall buy you on one condition."

Mike's ears perked up. Although he had rejected her product, she might buy his. "That would be wonderful," he said gratefully.

"Yes, I shall buy you and your product only if it can repair a broken heart." Ann was on the verge of tears. Mike had hurt her, but he realized—as did she—that all lasting relationships are built on truth and honesty. If he had "bought" Ann just to patronize her, she might have felt discounted and resentful.

Mike's response was immediate. "I am not designed to repair broken hearts, only to repair viral infections, but I think I can rewrite the program to include broken hearts as well."

122   Couples at the Crossroad

"In that case," replied Ann, "I shall not only buy you, I shall also recalibrate myself—as a relaxation rifle—so that I can shoot real bullets just in case the 'Kill 'em with kindness' approach won't work."

Mike was so relieved that he actually clapped his hands. They both had been able to sell themselves—and without too much compromising at that!

The most important result of this exercise is a greater awareness of one's self-image. The product you have created really does represent a truth about you and your lover. If, in your view, your lover does not want to buy the product, there is a very good chance that your lover does not want to buy you in real life either. This, of course, is a fantasy exercise: It reveals how you see yourself. If you are doing this exercise by yourself, note how much selling you have to do in order to get your imagined lover to buy you. Better yet, do the exercise again together with your lover, and share your responses. You can learn more about each other during this five-minute exercise than you can during a month of dates. If it turns out that neither of you can "sell" your respective products, it may be time to start questioning the viability of the relationship.

Exercise 5: Finger-Pointing

I next introduced the Finger-Pointer Exercise:

A common complaint we have about our lover is that he is so 'demanding.' The demands come out as finger-pointing words such as 'should,' 'ought to,' 'have to,' 'got to,' 'need to,' and 'must.' These words are generally designed to control people—through guilt, shame, or emotional bullying. The effects on people generally are the same: people end up feeling resentful and angry. The following exercise will help you get in touch with the quality of your partner's demands and expectations:

Find a comfortable place, settle in, and close your eyes. Imagine you are looking at yourself from above—from a vantage point that will reveal all your imperfections. See yourself sitting with your eyes closed. See what you are wearing; see your facial features, your clothing, and your posture. Imagine you have an x-ray machine that reveals your thoughts and feelings.

As you scan yourself, silently criticize what you see. Tell yourself what you should be doing or how you ought to behave in order to be accepted. Begin each sentence with 'You should…,' or 'You really ought to…,' or 'If you really want to be accepted, you must….' Listen to your voice, to the quality of your speech, as you recite the long list of complaints and criticisms. Is your voice harsh or helpful? As you recite these criticisms, become aware of your body. How do you respond to criticism?

Now, pretend that the demanding voice is the voice of your lover. Answer each should sentence you listed above. For example, looking down on yourself, you-as-your-lover might say, 'You should lose weight.' Answer this should with an "I" statement such as, 'I hate it when you tell me what to do!' Become aware of the kinds of feelings that are aroused.

Consider the words you use to answer your lover's criticisms. Are they the same ones you use in real life?

Ann's reaction was immediate and a bit frightening. "As I scanned myself," she said, "the word 'foolish' kept popping up in my mind. I saw myself dressed casually, trying to write. The demanding voice said, 'If you really want me to accept you, you must cut out that foolishness. Get a real job. Take care of your chores here at home. You need to grow up. You need stop being so spoiled.' The voice just wouldn't stop badgering me. Come to think of it, that voice has badgered me for years!"

Mike became alarmed. "You do not mean to say that you think I'm badgering you or making demands." His head dropped to his chest.

"No, not you, Mike. The same voice seemed to belong to two different people, I think. It was my father's voice when he became angry with my mother, and it was my ex-husband's voice when he became angry with me. Both of them were constantly criticizing and telling us what we *should* be doing."

Mike looked relieved and concerned at the same time. I suggested that Ann make a list of "should" statements and say them out loud. The task took only a second. The "shoulds" had been in her mind for years and years just ready to pop out.

"Ok," she said, "the critical voice says 'You should take better care of the house. You should stop writing and get a part time job to help pay the bills. You should go to the gym and do aerobics.'"

"And what do you say in response?"

"I feel like crying. I do not want to fight. I do not want to say what I'm really thinking. I loved my father and I loved my ex-husband when we first met. I do not want to tell them how I feel."

"But, Ann, if it somehow affects us, then you do have to confront those nasty voices." Mike was sitting next to her now, his hand on her hand.

"Ok...I want to say to both of them, 'What right do you have to tell me—or my mother—what to do. I hate you when you say those things. I want you out of my life. I want to destroy you when you criticize me like that. You are a pompous elitist ass. I will write when and what I want to write. I will wear the clothes I

124   Couples at the Crossroad

want to wear. I will eat chocolate Sundays until I weigh a thousand pounds if I want to. I'll have no more *shoulds* or *have-to's* from you, or you're fired from my life." She suddenly became very quiet.

Mike, brave soul that he was, tried to break her mood with humor. "Ann, dear," he said, "I love when you are so direct. But, really, don't you think you *should* have said it a long time ago?"

"*Should!*" she responded through gritted teeth. Ann was ready to pounce on him…until…until she took a closer look at the man she loved, and found that he was smiling. Her anger melted and she held his hand more tightly.

Mike's experience was no less profound. As he scanned his body, he heard the critical voice clearly and sharply say, "If you want me to accept you, you have to be a man! Straighten out those shoulders. Think, think, think! Big boys do not cry." The voice was relentless. Every time Mike heard the voice, he winced as though each word and each demand had a pointy barb that dug into his flesh.

When I asked him respond to the voice, he nearly screamed, "I do not have to listen to you anymore. You're dead!" Tears formed in the corners of his eyes as he explained that the voice belonged not to his father, but rather to his mother! While his father had apparently established the rule that logic and manliness excluded emotions, it was his mother who seemed to enforce the rule of the house. This was confusing to him. At a conscious level he did not remember her behaving in that way. He remembered only the sweetness and the support. Mike did not remember how his mother reacted to his temperament and to his early demands for attention. Nor should he have remembered since he was only toddler. By the time he entered school, he had learned the lesson very well: He kept his mouth shut, his ears open, and let the voice of the critical parent control his emotions. When I asked what he might do to rid himself of the voice, Mike's response was, "Nothing at all. My mother was a wonderful woman. She got her voice from her mother and from my father, and she passed it down to me. Now that I'm aware of it, I need to be responsible for my actions and my feelings. My mother's not here, my father's not here, and it's time for me to return their critical voices to the grave. I still love them. They nourished me with good training, good genes, and enough intelligence to make life relatively easy for me. But I need to throw out some of the bad voices before they ruin the happiness I've found here with Ann."

Exercise 6: Yes/No

The follow week I introduced Exercise #6 with the following instructions:

The past always seems to be with us. Memories invade our consciousness and disrupt our thoughts and feelings. But these memories are always imperfect recordings of past events. They are merely the "map," not the "territory."

Nonetheless, memories are useful to us because they contain clues to some unfinished business we need to complete before we can relegate it to the trash heap. This is especially true of bad memories and nightmares. Helping you finish a bit of unfinished business is the objective of the following exercise. It is a particularly important exercise because learning to complete thoughts, actions, and feelings is an absolutely essential ingredient in a healthy relationship.

Find a comfortable position. Lie back with your eyes closed. Direct your attention to your inner world, the world bodily sensations. Focus on your breathing. Inhale for four seconds, pause for four seconds, exhale for four seconds, and pause for four seconds. Continue this pattern of breathing until your mind begins to wander.

Remember a time when you were with your lover, a time when you said "Yes," but you really wanted to say "No." Visualize the event vividly; see it as though it were happening right here, right now. How are you dressed? Where are you? Notice anybody who might be in the area. Develop a clear picture of the surroundings.

Now turn your attention to the precise moment when you said "Yes." What does your voice sound like? Is it submissive, frightened, angry, or aggressive? Say "Yes" again in the same way you said it before. Become aware of any discomfort or tension.

What do you avoid by agreeing to do something you do not want to do? What do you gain? Go back to the moment just before you said "Yes." This time, say "No." Do you notice any change in your breathing, any hesitations, any tensions? Keep repeating the word "No" until you feel as though your lover has really heard you and understands what you mean. Create a dialogue in your mind. Tell your lover why you need to say, "Yes" when he demands something from you. Tell him why you are afraid to be honest with him.

Now, play the role of Mike (Ann). How do you experience being told "No?"

Continue the dialogue, switching roles after each response. When you become the other person, use your imagination to help you imitate his/her voice, body posture, and mannerisms. Notice how the two voices interact. Note any annoyance, arguing, resignation, cooperation, or fear. Finally, what do you think would happen if you, in real life, were to stop being a phony, and instead tell each other exactly how you feel? Take a few minutes to absorb what you have experienced. Then tell yourself a truth about your relationship. Use the first person, present tense, as though your lover were here with you now. For example, one truth might be: "I always say "Yes" to you because I'm afraid you'll leave me (yell at me, think I'm stupid, etc.).

126   Couples at the Crossroad

Ann's response: "I do not ever remember feeling that I couldn't tell Mike 'No' about anything. We have a great relationship, an honest one. However, I do remember when I was married to my first husband I said 'Yes' to virtually everything. And every time I said 'Yes' to things I did not want to do, I would become physically ill—nauseated really—by the thought that I would go along with whatever he wanted me to do even though I knew better. Yet when I even thought of saying 'No' I became so frightened that he would turn away from me—leave me on my own—that I cowered in the corner for the five years of our marriage. I remember one time when he 'requested' that I stay home while he went to his college reunion. I of course said, 'OK'. What I really wanted to say was, 'You're my husband and my place is by your side.' I couldn't say that. I couldn't even think it. Every time I said, 'No', I began to shake. I guess the truth of it is that I felt like the little girl my parents taught me I should always be. It wasn't until I went through a lot of therapy before I realized I can say 'No' any time I want without the world caving in on me."

Mike's response was different. "I do not remember saying 'Yes' too often actually. I seemed to always say 'No' but I act 'Yes.' My mother would always tell me how stubborn I was, but the truth of the matter was that I could never behave contrary to my parents' wishes. When I did do what I really wanted to do, I felt so guilty about disappointing them that I spent days in my room by myself, being afraid to come out lest they reject me totally. If I could do it all over again, I would say to them, 'When I say 'No' I mean 'No' and I won't be bullied by you any more. Being fair, I have to say my parents never bullied me at all. *I* bullied me and I tried to bully them by threatening to reject them if they asked too much of me. That's my truth: I can be a bully and I do not like that part of me at all."

Mike's recollection struck a nerve. Ann told him, "Every once in a while I see the bully side of you and I do not like it, but I accept it because I know you love me, and because—with all of your blustering—you are still the most kind and generous human I've ever known."

I selected this particular exercise because unfinished feelings and phoniness—emotional dishonesty—interfere with communication, spontaneity, and harmonious relationships. Participants often have much emotional energy invested in the event they choose to remember, and energy invested in a phony "Yes" can't be invested in other, more necessary activities. By re-experiencing the event clearly and totally in the present, by identifying with the parts of the situation they had chosen to avoid, Ann and Mike created an opportunity to become aware of the feelings and thoughts, which needed to be finished in order to have peace of mind. With this awareness, they could then decide whether they wanted to keep the undigested memory or to regurgitate it and toss it away along with other emotional debris—a decidedly better solution in the long run.

The other important aspect of the exercise was that Ann and Mike could now appreciate more fully the "truth" that prevented them from being totally honest in their relationships. We comply with the demands of others for many reasons—generally, to be accepted, to be loved, or to avoid conflict. There are any number of us who want to seduce others into believing we are "kind" or "nice." But always there is a price to pay. Sometimes it's worth it and sometimes it's not. The price for most of us is too dear: dishonesty, resentment, and ultimately self-contempt. However, saying "No" to every provocation is not the answer. The oppositional person is just as trapped as the person who always yields. Again, it is a matter of balance. Balance, in this case, revolves around a consideration of the demands of the situation. The objective is to be neither master nor slave.

Exercise 7: Have To/Choose To

Responsibility in a relationship means response-ability, the ability to respond to the demands of the environment while at the same time considering your own personal needs. Avoiding responsibility for how we behave, how we think, and how we feel offers short term relief but long term pain. The pain derives from the confusion and anxiety we experience when our ability to respond with intimacy and truthfulness has been compromised.

I asked Ann and Mike to do the following:

Make a list of five things you "have to" do in order to maintain your relationship (e.g., "I always have to give in," "I always have to make love when I'm not in the mood," "I always have to pay the bills," etc.). In your mind, say each of the statements on your list three times, each time with more intensity. Appreciate how your voice sounds. Is the voice whiny, angry, irritated, or submissive?

Now go back to the list of "have to's" and substitute the words "choose to." Again, repeat each statement three times, each time becoming more involved, more intense. As you repeat each statement, become aware of your bodily sensations, tensions, and feelings. Notice what happens when you change "have to" to "choose to." Most people report there are greater feelings of control—over the power to make choices, even unpleasant ones.

128   Couples at the Crossroad

Ann's recollection of her list of "have to/choose to" statements created feelings of anger, sadness, and fear. At first she was reluctant to tell Mike, but with his reassurance she courageously produced the five statements:

"I always have to be happy when I do not really feel that way."
"I always have to nearly beg you to tell me what's on your mind."
"I always have to think about how you'll feel if I do not say the right thing,"
"I always have to give up my writing time to accommodate your talking time."
"I always have to be gentle to avoid hurting your feelings."

Reciting each item on the list, Ann became increasingly more uncomfortable. Her breathing became labored. She perspired. Her eyes darted around the room in what appeared to be an attempt to avoid eye contact. Her voice quavered. And she finally became so nervous she refused to go on.

I asked her to now face Mike and tell him how she felt when she changed the words "have to" to "choose to." Her posture and facial expressions visibly changed. She appeared to be more confident. Her voice became stronger and her eye contact was sharp and focused.

"I choose to be happy when I do not really feel like it because I know it pleases you. It's a small sacrifice for seeing you happy."

"I choose to beg you to tell me what's on your mind because, although I know it bugs you, just getting any reaction from you is better than having to suffer the silence. I first noticed this when I was a little girl. I always seemed to need to know how my father was feeling, or rather how he was feeling toward me. He was always moody, and I never knew exactly what was going on inside him. It seems now that, as a little girl, I myself couldn't exist without acknowledgement by my father. I did not seem to have as much trouble with my mother. She always recognized me and my accomplishments."

"I choose to think about how you'll feel if I say the wrong thing. But I do not like it one bit! I want you to be pleased with me. I do not want to make waves and ruin the best thing that has ever happened to me, so I'm really careful, and I choose to be careful. It is draining though and I wish we could correct that somehow. I hope I'm not saying the wrong thing!" (Ann smiled at the irony of what she had revealed.)

"I choose to give up my writing time to accommodate your talking time. Getting you to talk any time is a gift!"

"I choose to be gentle so that I do not hurt your feelings. I like being gentle with you. I want you to secure and to know that I would never deliberately hurt

Exercises in Awareness 129

you. Having to be gentle isn't always easy. Actually, it becomes burdensome at times, especially when I become angry with you for some reason. And it's always hard for me balance my need to let you know that I'm angry at my need—oops, my choice—to be gentle. Overall though I'm much happier and I think you're much happier when I can be soft and gentle."

Mike read his list of five items slowly and carefully. Even now, he could not bring himself to say anything to displease Ann. I urged him to continue.

"I always have to figure out what mood you're in."

"I feel I always have to walk on eggshells so that I do not chance hurting your feelings."

"I always have to pretend that I'm listening to you when I really want to read the newspaper."

"I always have to go to your parents with you when I would much prefer to go to the theater or even go fishing with the boys (Ann's two sons by her first husband)."

"I always have to say I'm sorry even though I do not think I've done anything wrong."

Asked to change "have to" to "choose to," Mike looked directly into Ann's eyes. He took a deep breath, smiled briefly, and told her:

"I choose to figure out what mood you're in because I've learned how to deal with your mood swings and it just makes life easier for both of us."

"I choose to walk on egg shells. It's pretty tedious most of the time and sometimes I resent it because it's so emotionally draining. But it does let you know that I love you and I'm willing to be sensitive to your needs. In the general scheme of things, it's a pretty small price to pay."

"I choose to pretend to listen to you because I know you pretend to listen to me sometimes. It seems like we made some kind of deal months ago when we first began to see each other; I listen to you and you listen to me—out of affection and respect, if not always out of interest.

"I choose to go to your parents with you because, although I like my alone time, I actually do enjoy talking with your father. Maybe what I should do is invite him to go fishing with me and leave you and your mother to shop or talk or gossip." (Ann nodded approvingly.)

"I choose to say I'm sorry even though I do not think I've done anything wrong because I've learned that saying I'm sorry is really like saying, 'I love you.' You like to hear that and I like to say that, so why not?"

The session ended with a hug and a smile. What better ending could we have had?

130   Couples at the Crossroad

When we *have to* do something, more often than not, we are merely playing Svengali with ourselves. We certainly do not "have to" remain in a relationship that is poorly suited to our temperament, our sense of what is right and what is wrong, or our priorities in life. We may "choose to" because the relationship offers companionship, security, or because the neighbors might talk. But we do not "have to" stay in the relationship—at least in most cases. The important thing is to appreciate how we ourselves often limit our options in life, and then blame our lover so that we can justify our lack of responsibility, that is, our lack of response-ability: the ability to respond to the real demands of our life circumstance.

Exercise 8: Fears/Wishes

Most of us walk around with emotional splinters that insinuate themselves into every aspect of our lives at home, at work, and at play. Sensitive to their stings, we hesitate to make full contact with the people around us. These emotional splinters create a phobic attitude that reactivates memories from an earlier time in our lives. Unless we can convert these fears into desires, we become slaves to the ogres and witches called self-doubt and insecurity.

I asked Mike and Ann to try the following exercise because I wanted them to (re)discover how fear can be turned into desire. The exercise is difficult because it requires participants to take full responsibility for their behaviors and their vulnerabilities no matter how alien these behaviors appear to be.

Find a comfortable position and close your eyes. Imagine a place about three inches behind your eyes in what you might consider the center of your mind. When you have found the place most comfortable for you, picture Mike (Ann). Now list five things about your partner you are afraid of, e.g., "I'm afraid you'll reject me," "I'm afraid you will find me unattractive," "I'm afraid I will embarrass you," etc.

I gave Mike and Ann ten minutes to think of a list of fears and then asked them to write them down.

Ann's list:
I'm afraid you'll leave me for a younger woman.
I'm afraid that you will forbid me to write.
I'm afraid you'll think I'm a bad homemaker.
I'm afraid you won't talk to me when I do something wrong.

Exercises in Awareness 131

I'm afraid I'm not brainy enough for you.

Mike's list:
I'm afraid I won't live up to your expectations.
I'm afraid you will think I'm silly when I'm trying to be romantic.
I'm afraid you will think I would be a poor father.
I'm afraid you'll think I'm a clumsy lover.
I'm afraid I won't be sensitive to your feelings.

Now go back to the list of five things. Substitute the words "wish" or "desire" for the word "afraid." As you repeat each sentence, list the reasons why your fears might, in fact, be wishes. For example, "I wish you would reject me so I would have an excuse to (run away, stop working so hard, go out and have a drink)." Compare and appreciate the differences and similarities between your fears and your wishes. Listen carefully to your list of fears. Do you sound frightened? Do you sometimes feel you are manipulating your lover with your insecurity? What do you avoid by maintaining the victim's position? What do you avoid by not expressing your wishes and desires?

Ann's responses:

"I wish you would leave me for a younger woman. If you did, I would not have to worry about your rejecting me when I get older and I lose my looks. At least I would know you had a reason for leaving me and that you did not just hate me or find me revolting.

I wish you would forbid me to write. Sometimes I just get so tired having to produce chapter after chapter for my publisher. It would be a great relief if you could forbid me to write and let me spend more time with you and my children.

I wish you would think I'm a bad housekeeper. That way, I would not have to keep up the pretense that I like doing housework. I think it's drudgery—the ironing, washing the floors, making the bathrooms spic and span so that I can impress people with a skill I really do not want. Why don't we just get a house cleaner to come in once a week to do that sort of stuff? My, oh my, I wonder why I never thought of it before!

I wish you wouldn't talk to me when I do something wrong. I feel so guilty when things do not go well that I really do not want to look at you or talk to you. Why don't we make a pact? When I screw up, you give me a few hours to wind down and then you can tell me either that you're angry, or that you still love me, or both!

132   Couples at the Crossroad

I wish I weren't brainy enough for you. The truth is I think I'm pretty smart. But if I weren't, I wouldn't be so intimidating. I just want to be soft, sweet, and caring. But every once in a while the brain gets revved up and I can't stop myself from being smart! The best thing you can do is give me a big hug and a kiss and just tell me how beautiful you think I am even though I'm being a wise guy."

Mike's responses:

"I wish I couldn't live up to your expectations. It's like your feeling about writing. I sometimes get exhausted trying to measure up. I do not even know what I'm measuring up against anymore. I just know I have to be on my best behavior. Dot the *I*s and cross the *T*s. It's almost like living with my parents. I know you've never asked me to be this way, so I guess it's something in me that I have to conquer—or at least learn to live with.

I wish you would think I'm silly when I'm trying to be romantic. Not that I want to be silly at all. I just want to be able to loosen up. Be goofy if I want to be. Hug you and love you if I want without having to feel that there's a proper way of doing things—even being romantic.

I wish you would think I am a poor father. I do not feel comfortable with your children yet and I do not know how they feel about me. If you could convince them that I'm a complete ignoramus about fatherhood, it would be much easier for me and for them. We would all know what to expect. The truth is I love children and I think your kids are great. I'm sure I'm more than adequate at fatherhood, but it would be so much easier if I did not have to go through this breaking in period with your children and your entire family.

I wish you'd think I'm a clumsy lover. If you did, I wouldn't have to worry about not pleasing you. You would just assume that I'm not very good at sex and adjust your expectations. Yipes! There I go with my expectations again! Actually I love making love with you, but if you thought I were clumsier, you might become more assertive, and I think I would like that—at least on occasion.

I wish I wouldn't be so be sensitive to your feelings. I worry that I'll hurt you or make you sad or unhappy. I couldn't bear it if I did that. Sometimes I'm so sensitive to what you're feeling that I can actually feel the same thoughts and feelings myself. It gets in the way—not often but sometimes—because I can't tell you what I need to tell you in order to make necessary changes."

The "Fear/Wish" exercise revealed some of the more vexing thoughts Ann and Mike had. Not that any of the fears were in and of themselves very important, but together the fears had put pressure on the couple and made them feel uneasy. By confronting themselves with their own fears and converting them into wishes and desires, Ann and Mike gave themselves permission to be themselves, to demand the conditions that would make them happy with themselves and with each other. As it turned out, all of the fears were discussed fully and completely. The unfinished feelings that had lingered on—from childhood in several cases—were recognized and dealt with. As Mike pointed out, however, many of the feelings did not reflect trouble with the relationship per se. If they had, the fears, with the proper attention, could have been vanquished without difficulty. What made it hard for Ann and Mike were the voices of the critical parent that their minds couldn't let go.

There are legitimate instances when fear is the only appropriate response to a particular situation. The importance of the exercise, however, lies in our penchant for fooling others and ourselves by refusing to accept responsibility for what we really think and feel. "Fear" is often used as a tool to manipulate others into untenable positions. "Fear" might lead to submissiveness on our part and consequently bossy behavior or domination on our lover's part. Our lover's reaction then becomes a reason for us to withdraw from the relationship, to withhold affection or sexual contact, or to file for divorce. And all of this unpleasantness could be avoided by our being responsible for our fears and wishes.

The wish and the fear, as Freud pointed out, may be the same. It is the wise person who can discern the dis/advantages of acknowledging the two sides of the same mind.

Exercise 9: Make-A-Sandwich

The "Make-A-Sandwich" exercise is an extremely powerful if somewhat offbeat approach to self-awareness. I handed Ann and Mike paper and pencil and asked them to complete the following activity:

As part of your training in awareness, I want to suggest the following exercise. Imagine that Mike (Ann) is a...sandwich. (I know it's silly but trust me on this one). What kind of sandwich would he be? Take a bite of the imaginary sandwich. How does it taste? Spicy? Bland? Fatty? Tough? Stringy? Sweet? _____

After you taste the sandwich, chew it slowly and swallow it carefully noting the various tastes and textures. How do you experience swallowing (e.g., does it go down easily get stuck in your throat, feel satisfying, give you a too-full or too-empty feeling, etc.)?

Do you feel nourished and satisfied, or rather that there is something missing?

The exercise was wildly successful. Ann marveled at the kinds of images and sensations she conjured up while eating a "Mike sandwich." Mike *oohed* and *aahhed* while making munching noises. They seemed to be enjoying the adventure.

Here's how Ann experienced the "Mike sandwich:"

"Well, to be honest, I thought the whole idea was bizarre. Then I became intrigued by the possibilities. The sandwich was wonderful. It tasted like roast beef, a bit on the rare side with a luscious au jus that dripped through the bread. It was so tender that it dissolved as soon as I bit through the bread. Yet, it had substance, and the taste was almost sweet and languished in my mouth. I found the whole experience sexy in a strange sort of way. Each bite lasted only a few seconds before I swallowed it. It went down easily and filled me completely. But I craved more. It really was exactly how I experience Mike in real life. Gentle and sweet and sexy and yet he is a man of substance."

Mike was more restrained in his descriptions; nonetheless, he also seemed to have a good time with the activity.

"My sandwich was presented beautifully on a crystal plate with slices of tomato on the side. I really couldn't recognize what it was made up of. I'm not sure it was meat, but I'm not sure it wasn't. I do know that it tasted wonderfully dainty and yet it was filling. The taste was so concentrated that a tiny bite left an explosion of taste in my mouth. The texture was not at all chewy. The taste of the 'Ann sandwich' was so powerfully concentrated, only a small amount was necessary to fill me up. Her sweetness, daintiness, and power all mixed together in my mouth created a sensation unlike any I've ever experienced before. Even though I haven't a clue what it was that I was eating, I know that I want more, and that is an exact picture of what Ann is! Powerful, mysterious concentrated, intense, filling, and dainty. All the words describe her beautifully. The only thing I can add is that it also describes our relationship beautifully."

Our fantasies often reveal moments of truth. Only by acknowledging the powerful message that each truth delivers can we ensure the integrity of the relationship. In many ways, our fantasies and the truths they encapsulate are the true directors of the life script each of us has written many years ago. They tell us how to interpret the world beyond the skin boundary. They direct the cameras and the lighting of the inner world; they reflect the attitudes, the picture-thoughts, and the feeling tones that enhance—or detract—from the act of coupling with our lover.

Exercise 10: Expanding Your Boundaries

Falling in love is an intense but limited sort of intimacy. The sharpness of the experience brings excitement, and the excitement produces an ambiance of trust. The trust is limited, however, because time and experience have not tested it.

Being in love clearly is a different event. We have seen our lover in a variety of situations—when she is angry, sad, or embarrassed. Despite the discomfort, we continue to accept her uncritically over a relatively long period. The difference lies in the level of intimacy, the shared boundaries we enjoy. With intimacy, we not only survive, but we thrive happily!

I designed the following exercise (1) to help Ann and Mike learn how to expand their contact boundaries, and (2) to help them assess the nature of their "intimacy." The results of the exercise would provide important information to consider when they were ready to make their decision about staying together.

Music was essential for the first part of the experiment. Certain kinds of rhythms, instruments, and pitch enhance relaxation and increase alpha brain wave patterns. Together, the relaxation, and the alpha rhythms encourage creativity and intuitive thinking. The most effective music includes string and piano instrumentals that have a slow and steady beat. Baroque music is particularly well suited for this kind of exercise. (Kanon played by the pianist George Winston on the Windham-Hill label is an excellent choice.)

I told Ann and Mike:

Breathe rhythmically in time with the music: inhale four beats, pause four beats and exhale four beats. Do this until you discover tingly sensations on your finger tips, the tip of the nose, on lips, and on cheeks.

Become aware of your bodies, beginning with the toes, and slowly work up your body until you reach the scalp area. Your job is to become aware of the differences between what is occurring within your body and what was occurring outside your body. For example: inside, you might hear your heart beating while outside you might hear the traffic. Inside, you might experience a tingly feeling on your fingertips; outside, you might feel your feet on the floor. The objective is to develop an awareness of your skin as a boundary between you and the rest of the world, to discover the place that marks the difference between the you and the non-you.

Now "push" the boundary out a quarter of an inch at a time with each exhalation. Imagine that your skins—your contact boundaries—are like balloons that expand as you breathe out. Do this until you were able to push the boundary out about three feet in all directions.

136   Couples at the Crossroad

Now imagine that your contact boundaries merge. Experience the bodily sensations of the expanding boundaries as well as the emotions you feel.

Does merging with the other person feel comfortable? Intrusive? Do you begin to feel a sense of invasion? Do you experience a sense of resisting the merging? Or rather, do you feel a sense of oneness?

It turned out that Ann and Mike were entirely comfortable being in each other's "space." Neither one experienced a sense of intrusion or invasion. Each experienced a sense of *merging* with the other and then a sense of *freedom*. They left the office hand-in-hand and smiling. It was a beautiful session.

12

Dream Come True

The most powerful form of fantasy comes in the guise of dreams. Dreams serve many purposes, most of which are poorly understood. What we can say with some certainty, however, is that dreams and nightmares contain within them the seeds of truths that are powerful enough to change our thoughts, our feelings, and our actions. These nightly visitors are so powerful, they can create, sustain, and even destroy relationships.

A Leg

"A leg."

The words belonged to a woman who called me two days before a dream seminar.

She continued, "Can we talk about it now, or would you rather we wait until Thursday's dream workshop?"

I was too intrigued to wait.

"A leg?" I asked.

"Yes, that's right, doc, I dreamt of a leg."

"And what was this leg doing?" I inquired.

"It wasn't doing anything. It was just a leg," the woman answered.

Now I was puzzled. What could a "leg" possibly mean?

The truth is we can go around and around looking for the "meaning" of dreams and possible symbolism. Sometimes—to paraphrase Freud—a leg is just a leg. Nonetheless, I persevered.

"You dreamt about a 'leg.'"

"Yes, I think I might have been in the shower, and there was the leg."

"Would you please *be* the leg in the dream for a moment and tell me what you experience?"

"You want me to *be* the leg? OK, I'm the leg. No, no, I do not want to ever be that leg!"

"What do you experience as the leg?"

"I have psoriasis and I'm ugly and no man will ever want to be with me."

It turned out that the woman had a Saturday night date with a new gentleman friend and she was distraught by the thought that her skin condition would turn him off. No matter how many showers she took, the fear that psoriasis would appear at an inopportune time took control of her thoughts.

I do not know what happened on her date, but the woman did show up at the dream workshop two days later. When I asked for a volunteer to share his/her dream, the woman raised her hand. "And what did you dream?" I asked.

Her response: "Fingernails."

"Fingernails?" I asked.

"Yes, and I can't decide on what color to paint them."

This time I did not bother with the role-playing. I had a hunch the dream was about men and her indecisiveness ("I can't decide on what color to paint them"). I asked, "And which man do you want to kick out of your life."

She took a deep breath and finally said, "John...I'm dying of boredom!"

In this particular case, the dream represented a particular "existential" truth ("I'm dying of boredom"). In other cases, dreams do not.

The line separating sleep and wakefulness is vague and elusive. Subjectively, there often is no difference between the two states. Dream-like feelings intrude into the waking state and external stimuli often insinuate themselves into the sleeping state. There appears to be a permeable membrane between the two states with fuzzy feelings and sensations passing subtly and at times imperceptibly from one state to the other. An external conflict might present itself as a simple picture-thought without any real words attached (for example, a "leg") or an internal dream-like event might present itself in the waking state as an irrational and poorly understood behavior (for example, the psychotic thinking and behavior of schizophrenics).

The importance of dreams and nightmares in our daily life is unmistakable. They tell us things we do not want to hear. They force us to pay attention to aspects of our lives that are secret to our conscious minds.

For example, research has suggested that dreams can reveal physical illness before the symptoms appear. In one dream, the dreamer, a physician, saw someone mugging a patient of his in the street. Lying beside the patient was a kidney totally detached from the body. Shortly after the dream, the physician learned that he himself had an infected kidney that required care.

Likewise, *curing* illness through dreams has been documented by many researchers and clinicians. Reportedly, after Alexander the Great dreamed of a dragon with a plant in its mouth, he sent his soldiers to the location of the plant specified in the dream. The story goes that the soldiers retrieved the plant, which was then used to cure Alexander's ailing friend, Ptomemaus.

The relationship between what we dream and how we behave is fascinating. It is as though one part of us tells another part of us a deep secret that describes who we are and what we fear/wish most in the world.

Dreams—Then and Now

It wasn't really until Freud in the late 1800s began to tinker with the possibilities of an "unconscious" mind that the import of dreams was finally realized by the industrialized world.

The early researchers were mainly interested in the cultural and anthropological aspects of dreams. Dreams in their view became the history of culture. The universality of dream symbols strongly suggested that cultural bias played a major role in the interpretation of dreams. While Freud's approach incorporated the symbolism of nightly events such as dreams, he appeared to be more concerned with dreams as a history of the individual rather than as the history of the race or the culture.

Early Greek philosophers on the other hand saw dreams as messages from the gods; others, including Buddhists, felt that life itself—what we call "reality"—was simply another form of a dream from which we will eventually awaken.

Psychoanalysts in the 1920s were partial to the idea of dreams as reflections of strong conflicts in our waking life, not just sexual conflicts often suggested in the writings of Sigmund Freud. More recently, dream workers have developed the notion that dreams are "existential" messages that succinctly state who and what we are, what we're afraid of, whom we're angry at, and what kinds of emotional conflicts we are confronting right now—at this moment.

Dreams may also be viewed as projections of a fragmented personality whose pieces vie for recognition and completion. Many psychoanalysts maintain that dreams are meant to be communications between the individual and the important people around him, revealing for example the true feelings patients have toward their therapists.

Dreams as "unfinished business" was a theory favored by Gestalt Therapists at the time when the Human Potential Movement (1960s and 1970s) had gained popularity as a way of empowering people who were experiencing an absence of

140   Couples at the Crossroad

social connection. They emphasized the need to "complete" unfinished feelings and worked with the personality fragmentation often found in dream material.

Whether we believe that dreams are reflections of existential messages and godliness, or the universality of dream symbolism, or even the seeds of cultural ritual, we are left with the impression that dreams are a reservoir of picture-thought-sensations that reveal our most intimate but subconscious awareness of the truths underlying our conscious behavior.

Our particular interest in dreams and nightmares centers around their potential for revealing emotional and sexual conflicts, issues with life and/or death, and uncompleted feelings related to anger, fear, and love. In short, we are interested in them because they reveal secret truths that influence our thoughts, our beliefs, and our decision-making.

Dreams as "Unfinished Business"

"Unfinished Business" refers to the biological and psychological need to bring closure to certain feelings and certain suppressed behaviors. Angry feelings demand that we redress the wrong—real or imagined—caused by other people or events. Sadness requires us to grieve for the lost object. Happiness does not feel right without a bounce in our step and a smile on our faces. All are examples of "unfinished business."

Most of us are not very aware of those kinds of feelings. They remain hidden because they are too dangerous to acknowledge. Little children, employees, spouses, and others engaged in the tricky business of getting along with people often can't voice their feelings or their thoughts because in their minds—and often in reality—the act would lead to abandonment, disapproval, or physical violence.

Among the feelings that we need to "finish," the ones that seem to occupy most of our time and most of our energy include: sexual conflict, anger, sadness, failure, fear, and joy—the very same feelings that dictate our behavior toward our lovers (and most other people in our lives).

The best example of a dream as "unfinished business" came unexpectedly from a man locked up in the sex offender unit at a large prison in New Jersey. The man had been arrested over a dozen times since 1929 for "molesting" young girls. At the time of his most recent arrest, he was a successful caterer, the owner of three profitable carwash businesses, and the respected deacon of his church. (All of this despite the fact that he had scored within the mentally deficient range on psychological testing!). Examining his record, I found that the man had often worked as a valet or butler for some of the more prosperous families in his community in Georgia. For reasons not yet clear, he seemed to be drawn to blond-haired, blue-eyed girls about eight years old. In most cases, the girls were also fond of him and came to regard him as a surrogate parent while their parents were away. He never physically harmed any of them, nor did he molest them in the usual sense, but he was compelled to pat them, stroke their arms, or touch their hair.

I was eager learn what unfinished business the man's compulsions represented. The man, called George, was also eager to discover why he got himself in trouble. A member of a therapy group, consisting of nine men, all convicted of sex crimes, George shot his hand up when I asked who wanted to "work."

I asked him to sit next to me. In front of him was an empty chair, a prop popularized by Gestalt Therapists at that time. George volunteered the following dream:

I was in a field with two girls. I was young, maybe five years old. One girl asked me to touch the other one. I did not want to do it, but she was bigger than me and I thought she would yell at me if I did not. Then I woke up.

I asked George to tell us what he remembered about growing up. Here's what he said:

My momma and me were living in a rich man's house in Georgia. This was a long time ago, back in the 20's. My momma cleaned the man's house and cooked for the family. The man had two daughters. One was eight years old and one was six years old. We played outside together all the time. Those were really happy times for me.

I asked George to describe the girls.

The six year old—her name was Abigail—she was always playin' and runnin' around. She liked me and we liked to swim down by the creek. Everything was fun until she went to school. I stayed at the house and helped my momma. The other girl—her name was Dolly—she was eight years old. She was real pretty. She had blonde hair and pretty blue eyes. I really liked her. I think she really liked me too.

I asked George to pretend that the older girl, Dolly, was sitting in the empty chair directly in front of him. "Tell *her* what you just told *us* about her. Make believe she's right here with us now."

142   Couples at the Crossroad

Without losing a beat, George began a dialogue with the young blonde-haired girl he was so fond of.

"I miss you, Dolly. Remember when you and me and Abigail were in the field. You told me to touch Abigail. I did not want to do it, but I did not want you to get mad at me. I really wanted to touch you, not her. I liked the way you looked and the way you treated me and my momma so good back in those days. I've been searching for you all over. I keep looking for your hair and your pretty eyes. I keep thinking that I see you, but then you turn into someone else and the police arrest me. Can't we be together again?" (Becomes very sad and tearful.)

I asked George to create a dialogue between Dolly and himself.

As Dolly: "George, you know I like you. We had good times in Georgia, but I can't be with you anymore. I'm an old woman. I'm married. I have five children and seven grandchildren."

As George: "But I do not want you to leave me."

As Dolly: "I need to say goodbye, George. We're both too old. You're married and I'm married and we need to say goodbye."

As George (tearful): "Please, Dolly, can't you stay for a little while more?"

As Dolly: "Goodbye, George."

As George (crying): "Please do not leave."

As Dolly: "Goodbye, George."

As George (shoulders back, taking a deep breath, looking at the ghost of Dolly's memory sitting in the chair): "Goodbye, Dolly."

George's "unfinished business" with blonde-haired eight-year-old girls was now complete. After a forty-year search, he finally found the girl of his dreams, and he could finally let her go.

Dreams as Part of the Grieving Process

Grieving means "letting go," and "letting go" means that we experience great sadness, anger, and helpless. The (impending) loss of a lover, a parent, a child, a job, or a movie hero/ine, leaves us feeling empty—a hard-to-describe feeling that most of us want to avoid. After all, "letting go" requires that we (re)experience a feeling of abandonment and aloneness—a life without a person (pet, hobby, job, affiliation) who has become part of our very being. Often nightmares accompany our losses, disguising them as losses easier to manage. Nonetheless, our sense of despair, sadness, and emotional turbulence lie just below the surface of our consciousness waiting to reveal themselves.

Jane was thirty-three years old when she joined a counseling group for volunteers at a drug rehabilitation center. The twelve members of the group were responsible for the hotline calls and follow-up services. On this particular evening, we were examining the nature of personal loss and how it affected our work with drug addicts.

Jane suggested that she had just gone through a separation from her husband of two years and offered the following dream fragment:

I was in my old house, walking up the stairs to the second floor bedroom. I noticed that the railing was missing...

I asked her to imagine that she was in the house now and to tell us what she was experiencing.

"I am very frightened. The house is old and empty, still attractive but old. I am all alone. There is no railing on the staircase and I am afraid I am going to fall down. That's all I can remember."

A part that is "missing" in our dreams is often found in another part of our lives. I asked Jane to tell the same dream fragment from the point of view of the missing railing.

"You can't see me because I'm not here anymore. You're frightened and you can't lean on me anymore." (Jane begins to sob.)

I asked her to become herself and to respond to the railing. "I'm scared. I need you. You always gave me strength. I could always count on you. I could always lean on you. Now you're gone. (Sobbing loudly) That was the last thing I told my husband before we decided to split up. I guess I still can't accept it."

Another woman recently told me the following dream:

I was real little. I was riding on the back of a puppy. She would carry me all over the house. She took care of me and was my best friend even though she growled a lot and liked to show me how sharp her teeth were. Then the scene changed. I was carrying the puppy, which was now an old dog, up a big hill. She still tried to growl but was old and all that came out of her mouth were little yippy sounds. I woke up crying.

I asked the woman to describe the scene from the point of view of the dog using the present tense.

"I like to carry the little girl around on my back. I can be grouchy but she likes me a lot and we have fun together. I like to show my teeth off. They are sharp. I do not hurt anybody and I'm not really trying to scare the girl. She is laughing and pulling at my ears. I do not mind because I know she loves me.

Now I am old. I have no energy. I am weak. I can't see. I can't walk. The little girl is now a grown woman and instead of me carrying her around, she's carrying me up a hill. I must be quite a burden but she seems to still love me just as I love her so she doesn't mind too much. She is very sad. I wish I could make her happy."

I asked the woman to create a dialogue between her and the dog.

As the woman: "I wish you felt better. I want you to be happy. You seem to be so tired and sad nowadays. But I'll carry you just as you carried me and took care of me."

As the dog: "I am very old. I'm sorry you have to carry me. I do not want to be a burden to you. Perhaps if you just let me lie down and rest on the side of the hill I'll feel better, and you won't have to carry me anymore."

As the woman: "I won't let you go. You are too precious to me. If I put you down you won't get up again…I just know it. I'll take care of you. Just hop in my arms and I'll carry you and we'll be together."

As the dog: "You can't take care of me anymore. It's time that you let me go, so you can find someone else to take care of. You need a husband and children. You must put down and let me sleep." (Woman is crying as she says these words.)

The woman continued the dialogue until she was able—at least in fantasy—to put the dog down. We talked about the woman's life and what might be troubling her at that time.

"I think I understand my dream now. The dog is my grandmother. She raised me when I was very young. She taught me how to sew, how to cook and how to bake, and she made sure I took my piano lessons. She was tough. She barked just like the dog in my dream. She took care of me and loved me more than anyone else in this world, including my parents.

"Now my grandmother is old. She volunteered to go into a nursing home not too long ago. She did not want to be a burden on anyone, she told us. I wanted to take care of her. I tried to persuade her that everything would be all right if she just wouldn't give up. She said she wasn't giving up. She was just tired and needed to rest, and that it would be helpful if I would just visit just once in a while and not be a pest about it. I finally gave in. I see her on occasion and write to her as often as I can. But how can I say goodbye to the most wonderful woman in the world. I feel empty just thinking about it. (Woman sobs for ten minutes before regaining her composure.) I guess I need to let her go. It's unfair. She never let me go, but I need to let her go." (More tears and more sadness).

Dreams as Existential Messages

Existential messages reflect our fears and wishes about life and death. They generally take the form of a statement describing the way we experience ourselves within our world right here and right now. The messages are powerful reminders of our mortality—our weaknesses and our strengths.

A gentleman of sixty years was recuperating from mitral valve replacement surgery. The operation, although successful, required extensive surgery. His chest had to be "cracked." His heart had to be pushed aside and repositioned. A major leg vein had to be removed and grafted to another blood vessel surrounding the heart muscle. Despite this, the gentleman claimed that he was regaining his strength and stamina and was very pleased with his progress.

His dream told a different story:

I'm opening the front door to my house. I find myself in a room that looks like a large foyer. The room is bare. To the left of the foyer is another large room, also bare—except for a few wall decorations and a window treatment. Directly ahead there is another room slightly elevated. Just in front of this room, however, there is some old furniture. There is no wall between the front room and the middle room.

I can see an old beat up sofa and pillows with stuffing spilling out. There are all kinds of debris on the floor—bits of paper, empty soda cans, newspaper all balled up. There is also a naked toddler running around, laughing and having a good time. He appears to be oblivious to the mess in his diaper, which has fallen down around his ankles.

In the back and to the right, there is a room full of people—strangers to me. They are watching old movies on an ancient screen, using one of those eight-millimeter projectors. The people are also having a good time. There is lots of smoke and a good bit of drinking along with the merriment.

I become very angry and I begin to shout, "What's going on in my house? What's going on in my house?"

Then I woke up, and I realized what's going on in "my house." The dream actually summed up exactly what I had gone through and what I was going through. "My house was a mess. It was in shreds." The reason for my surgery, I was told several weeks before, was that my mitral valve was "shredded." I also had debris in my body—a staph infection, small blood clots that affected my vision, and bits of residue from the surgery itself. The dream's message was clear to me. The truth was that I was the house. I was the mess!

When I told my daughter about this dream, her response was elegant: "Well, Dad, I guess you have to hire some people to clean up the house."

I replied, "That's exactly why I'm here in the hospital. I've hired the best house-cleaners (doctors) I could find."

The man's dream revealed the state of his health; it also revealed the state of his mind. Different parts of his personality were in conflict. The "owner" of the house was angry that there were intruders—microbes and illness—in his home and that his house was "shredded." Another part of him, represented by the toddler, was in a state of regressed oblivion. The people in the back room watching movies were the part of him that was entertaining (and being entertained by the) nurses, the hospital television, and all the "uninvited" guests who came to visit him.

I asked the man to create a dialogue among the different personality fragments. I suggested that he begin by retelling the dream from the point of view of the toddler.

"I am N___'s regressed self. He has just come into the house and seems to be mad that it's such a mess. In the back, a bunch of people are having a good time. I do not know who they, but they seem to feel pretty comfortable talking and laughing. They're watching old-fashioned movies. I see them smoking and drinking. They seem nice enough, but I wonder who they are. All around me is trash. The old couch is torn and the pillow stuffing has been pulled out and thrown on the floor. N___'s pretty mad about the trash and all the strangers in the back. I am not at all concerned about that stuff—or what is socially acceptable. I want to play and jump, and drag all these old blankets around with me. My diaper is messy, my hands are all sticky and dirty, but I do not care."

In reaction to the toddler's voice, the man responded:

"I want to get this place cleaned up. Soon you will be too old to act like an infant. It's easy for you to have that nonchalant attitude; you do not have to get out and make a living. Well, enjoy yourself now, because pretty soon you'll have to grow up and start taking care of yourself and your house."

In this brief encounter with himself, the man reveals how angry he is with his illness. He needs to remain in the hospital, accepting orders from doctors, nurses, and the support staff. He feels young and helpless. He wants to straighten things out, get better, get back to work, and take care of business. In the meantime, the regressed part of him appears to enjoy the freedom to be "messy." The carefree attitude is something that the adult part of the man does not tolerate easily.

I then asked the man to be the sofa—the part of him that feels "shredded":

Dream Come True   147

"I am the sofa. I'm not much to look at, but I'm still functional. The man who just walked through the front door will make sure that I get fixed someday, but right now I'm just feeling old and worn out. All around me people are having a good time. The people in the back room are enjoying a movie, good drinks, and chatting with each other. I hear a lot of laughing. The toddler is running all around. He's naked…doesn't have a care in the world. I wonder what it would be like to feel that."

As the toddler (to the sofa):

"Do not feel too bad. Things will change in time. The man will fix you and you'll feel better. I'll have to grow up and I won't be able to be so carefree. All things change with time." (Notice how the tone of the toddler's language has already changed.)

As the man responding to the sofa and the toddler:

"I guess I was hasty. I'm not angry anymore. I'll fix you (sofa) and I'll change your diaper (toddler) until you become more self-sufficient. I guess I have to accept you the way you are until I get my strength back. But what about those people in the back? Who are they?"

Man to the people in the back room:

"Who are you and how did you get in here? I hear you laughing and having a great time."

People collectively to the man:

"Come back here and join us. We'll wait for you. We have all the old movies you like. You can have a couple of beers if the doctor says it's ok, and you can make new friends. We're your past and your future. We live inside you the same way the sofa and the toddler live inside you. Do not be too angry with us."

As the man responding to the people:

"Well, I do not like the way you just seemed to show up, having a good time without me. I'm feeling pretty miserable and I do not need any reminders of how things ought to be."

People to man:

"Yes, we are reminders. This is what's waiting for you as soon as you get better. Be patient, sit it out for a few weeks and then come to visit. We'll try to keep the noise down, but we're going to be here just waiting for you. We're really looking forward to it."

All of the parts of the man's personality demanded attention—demanded to be heard. Like puzzle pieces, fragments of thoughts and feelings finally fit together to make up a complete picture or a *Gestalt*. The toddler—the happily regressed part of the man—resigns himself to growing up; the sofa asks for and

148   Couples at the Crossroad

receives help with repairs; and the people in the back agree to be patient while the gentleman heals after his surgery. And because of this, the man can at last feel at peace with himself and with the world within him.

Ann's Dream and Mike's Journey into Intimacy

Dreams magnify what we feel and experience at an unconscious level. They are like boulders lying under the surface of the water in a river. We can judge where the boulders are by the way the water parts slightly or forms a ripple, but we do not perceive the boulder themselves. By understanding the language of the river—by understanding the language of the dream—we begin to understand the basic needs, desires, fears, and angers that motivate our lovers and ourselves. More importantly, we begin to realize how to resolve emotional conflicts that play havoc with our relationships.

Because dreams offer incredibly powerful tools for understanding ourselves and our conflicts, they were the focus of our last session together. The goal was to help Ann and Mike bring to a close whatever misgivings they might have had about themselves, about their relationship, and about each other. This dream session, however, was different: I asked Ann and Mike to share and to work on *one* dream. We began with a dream fragment offered by Ann. I asked her to tell the dream in the first person, present tense, as though we were there in the dream with her:

Mike and I are in bed together. He has his back toward me. I'm feeling hurt and angry. Why is he turning his back on me? He seems to be preoccupied with something else. I stroke his hair. Still he doesn't move. I pull him toward me, but he seems to want no part of me. I am confused. What have I done wrong? What have I done wrong? I wake up crying (Ann begins to cry).

I asked Ann to create an ending for the dream:
"I have to wake up. It is too painful for me to feel this rejection from the man I love."
I repeat the request:
"Ok. Here goes. Mike turns away from me and I'm feeling hurt. I say, "What have I done wrong? Why don't you love me? He doesn't answer me. I poke him. Answer me! Why don't you love me? He still doesn't answer me. I punch him on the back and on the shoulders. He doesn't move. Then I notice that he is shaking, sobbing really. I am feeling very sad. What is wrong, I ask him. Why aren't

you talking to me? Why don't you love me? He continues to cry. He's not looking at me. He's turned over on his left side. I can't see his face. I want to see his face. I love him and I want to see his face."

I ask Ann to say this directly to Mike.

"I love you and I want to see your face. I do not want you to turn your back on me. I want to see your face. What have I done wrong? Why can't you love me the way I love you?"

Mike's response:

"But I do love you. I am listening to you and it breaks my heart that I can't show you the affection that you crave. I turn my back on you only because I do not want to see how sad you are. My mind and my body ache for you, and I do not know how to show it." (Tears)

I asked Mike to share Ann's dream, to enter it and to change the ending of the dream in any way he wants.

"I'm lying in bed with Ann. She snuggles up close to me, but my back is turned toward her. She wants me to hold her. I'm having trouble showing my affection. It makes me anxious to have someone that close to me emotionally. I never experienced that sort of thing growing up."

I point out that he is talking *about* the dream and not really experiencing it in the *now*. Again, I suggest that he can change the dream in any way he wants.

"OK. I am lying next to Ann. She is pulling me closer. I turn over and face her. I see her eyes. I touch her face. I smell her hair. She is very beautiful. I say to her, 'Will you marry me? And she says...I do not know what she says."

I said, "Ask her now, Mike. Ask her what she wants to do."

Mike turned toward Ann. Her face brightened.

"Ann, darling, you know I love you. I can't always show it, but my affection for you and the children is real. I want to be with you for the rest of my life. Will you marry me?"

Ann pulled him closer. Looking straight into his eyes, she said, "Of course I'll marry you. It's all I've thought about for the past six months."

The session ended. After giving me a warm handshake and expressing their gratitude, Ann and Mike left the office, walking arm in arm. I next heard from them two months later. Inside the invitation to their wedding was a handwritten note signed by both of them. The note said, "Thanks for helping us find the 'path with a heart.'"

13

Final Word

Loving is creative living, and the person in love is a person who creatively bridges the chasm between her and her lover. She creates harmonious separateness, a circumstance that enables two different people to behave as equals. This equality is the act of balancing and integrating interests, and caring for her lover in a way that ensures mutual abundance, as when Romeo says to Juliet, "The more I give, the more I have."

Loving/living is a matter of responsibility, care, respect, and knowledge. Responsibility is the ability to respond to our lover's needs and fears. Caring is the active and lively concern for our lover's spiritual growth. Respect is the appreciation of our lover's uniqueness. Knowledge is the full awareness that comes with intimacy, commitment, and passion.

Each of us ascends from the early narcissism of infancy to the capacity for loving our parents, our neighbors, our community, and finally our lover. The steps along the way provide us with more freedom, and, ironically, with a greater willingness to become more captive. The constant process of maturing, of unfolding our capacity for love, is crucial for the evolution of man as a social being. It becomes equally crucial for our own evolution as celebrants of life.

By this time, you have become intimately acquainted with your lover and with yourself as well. With each day, the kaleidoscope of your relationship turns slightly to reveal more beauty, more thoughts, more pictures, more beliefs, and more values, juxtaposing and adding intrigue and excitement to your time together.

It is my deepest wish that during your journey through these exercises, you have (re)discovered that your lover is the one who makes you happy now, and who will be there to make you happy in the future. Care, respect, knowledge, response-ability, and diligence on your part will increase the odds that the match is a good one. A nod to Providence wouldn't hurt at all.

APPENDIX A

The Decision Index

It's time to put these ideas to work. The vignettes below will introduce you to four married couples. Each couple completed the *Decision Index*. After examining each couple's responses, try to figure out whether (a) the couple stayed together (b) separated (c) divorced or (d) continued to see a therapist because "there's still hope we can make it work." As you read, think about your own relationship, its potential for success and its risk of failure. I provide an analysis of each couple's responses. Here is what the *Decision Index* looks like in its entirety:

Decision Index

Name _____ Date _____

Address _____

City _____ Zip Code _____

Telephone(s) Home _____ Work Number _____ Cell Phone _____

Email Address _____ Referred by _____

Reason for seeking counseling at this particular time

_____

_____

Directions: We designed these scales to help you make decisions about your relationship. Before completing the *Decision Index*, review the descriptions of the scales offered in the text. Respond to all items even though you may be unsure of your answers.

1. SIGNS of LOVE: When two people become a loving couple, they experience certain feelings and attitudes. Here are seven of them:

- They want exclusive companionship.

151

152   Couples at the Crossroad

- They want to share feelings, our thoughts, our experiences, and themselves.
- They learn how to give and take according to their needs, their energy, their generosity, and their assertiveness.
- They develop more trust.
- They learn to establish a balance between possessiveness and tolerance.
- They are willing to ensure their lover's safety and comfort to a greater degree than their own.
- They discover that sex is only one dimension of a three-dimensional love.

Indicate how many signs you and your lover share:

5 = We exhibit two or fewer signs
4 = We exhibit three signs
3 = We exhibit four to five signs
2 = We exhibit six signs
1= We exhibit all seven signs

2. BURDEN: Rate the burden carried by your lover during your courtship.

1 = No Stress
2 = Mild Stress
3 = Burdened But Manageable Stress
4 = Overburdened, Barely Manageable Stress
5=Always In Crisis, Generally Overwhelmed By Stress

3. TRAINER: Note whether your lover was trained by his/her Nurturing parent/caretaker, by a Critical parent/caretaker, or by a generally impersonal environment, that is, the "streets," or perhaps a foundling/foster home of poor quality. Use the following rating scale:

1 = Nurturing, Affectionate Care-Taker
2 = Critical, But Responsive Caretaker
3 = Antisocial/Gang Environment
4 = Cold, Unresponsive Care-Taker
5=Impersonal Asocial Environment

4. BONDING: Rate your lover's capacity for bonding, using the following scale:

1 = Strong "Normal" Capacity for Bonding
2 = Strong But Abnormal Attachment ("Too Close" To Family)
3 = Limited Capacity for Attachment
4=Extremely Difficult to Bond With
5 = Remains Totally Unbonded

5. RAPPORT: Review the important section on Rapport in Stage 1. Rapport, or the lack of it, is the ability to deepen a relationship over time. It is an immediate experience. We often get certain "vibes" within minutes of meeting someone. It is the first step toward a feeling of intimacy in that it involves the establishing of emotional comfort and the expansion of self-boundaries. We noted earlier that some people invite us into their worlds; others set up boundaries that keep us out. Still others have boundaries that vary in their permeability. Ideally, we want a lover who will welcome us in when we want to make a strong contact, and who will allow us to leave when the contact becomes too strong or uncomfortable.

Use the following scale to rate the level of rapport with your lover:

1 = Relationship Continues To Grow Each Day
2 = Relationship Grows Slowly But Perceptibly
3 = Relationship Is Deep But Has Reached A Static Point
4 = Relationship Changes Erratically
5 = Relationship Has Fizzled But I'm Too Scared to Move On

6. DESTRUCTIVE ATTITUDES AND BEHAVIORS: The harm caused by destructive behavior and negative attitudes cannot be overemphasized. The scale below points up a few of the many areas of conflict that harm relationships.

Destructiveness Scale

Determine how much damage your relationship has suffered because of harmful disagreements and behaviors using the following scale. Place a check mark on the line to the right of the item that best describes the degree to which each behavior/ attitude damages your relationship:

Couples at the Crossroad

	Degree of Harm to Relationship			
	Not Damaging		Very Damaging	
Behavior	**1**	**2**	**3**	**4**
1. Disagreement over $	___	___	___	___
2. Gambling	___	___	___	___
3. Absence from Home	___	___	___	___
4. Initiation of Sex	___	___	___	___
5. Frequency of Sex	___	___	___	___
6. Quality of Sex	___	___	___	___
7. Unfaithfulness	___	___	___	___
8. Jealousy	___	___	___	___
9. Impotence/Frigidity	___	___	___	___
10. Alcohol/Drug Abuse	___	___	___	___
11. Temper Outbursts	___	___	___	___
12. Physical Abuse	___	___	___	___
13. Nagging	___	___	___	___
14. Poor communication	___	___	___	___
15. Dependency/Parents	___	___	___	___
16. In-laws	___	___	___	___
17. No Mutual Interests	___	___	___	___
18. Selfishness	___	___	___	___
19. Clinginess	___	___	___	___
20. Lack of Friends	___	___	___	___
21. Child-Rearing Values	___	___	___	___
22. Different Religions	___	___	___	___
23. Lack of Trust	___	___	___	___
24. Lack of Respect	___	___	___	___
25. Political Differences	___	___	___	___

The Decision Index   155

On the scale below, indicate how much damage these behaviors and attitudes might have caused:

1=There Has Been No Damage
2=Damage Is Slight and Easily Repaired
3=Relationship Is Difficult But Differences Are Manageable
4=Relationship Is Extremely Uncomfortable But Worth Saving
5=Relationship Is So Damaged That There Is No Hope for Recovery

7.   PASSION-INTIMACY-COMMITMENT TRIAD: Most successful couplings depend on the compatibility of its members. Three-dimensional relationships require passion, intimacy, and commitment for enduring stability and excitement. Complete the 3-D Compatibility Scale as directed:

The 3-D Compatibility Scale

We designed the 3-D Compatibility Scale below to help you discover your attitudes, beliefs, and feelings about your lover and about various aspects of your relationship. To complete the scale, simply rate the degree to which you agree with each statement by filling in the spaces to the right of the statement. For example, in the column for item #1, you might rate "I love my lover so much that I am willing to sacrifice everything I own to make him safe and happy" a rating of "5" (Strongly Agree). In like fashion, complete the ratings for all twelve items.

After you have completed all the ratings, add up the numbers and interpret the total scores as instructed at the end of the exercise. The results will reveal how you perceive intimacy/passion/commitment—the three dimensions of love. The results also will give you a compatibility "profile" that might assist you in deciding whether you want to continue or terminate your relationship. Use the following code as a guide:

5 = Strongly Disagree, Not At All
4 = Disagree, Seldom
3 = About Average, As Much As Most People
2 = Agree, Often
1= Strongly Agree, Always
? = Do not know enough to rate this item

Item	Rating

1. My lover is the most sexually attractive person I know. _____

2. Sometimes I get so excited just thinking about my lover that I have trouble falling asleep at night. _____

3. I hate to admit it, but at times I feel overly possessive of my lover. _____

4. I love my lover so much that I am willing to sacrifice everything I own to make him safe and happy. _____

5. My lover and I share feelings and thoughts more than most other couples. _____

6. My lover and I feel so emotionally close that we feel and think like one person. _____

7. What I like best about my sexual relationship with my lover is the closeness and the tenderness. _____

8. I did not realize I was in love until I had known my lover for many months. _____

9. I often think about how my lover and I will look and feel together ten years from now. _____

10. "Until death do us part" is the most important part of the wedding vow. _____

11. The most important part of any relationship is total commitment. _____

12. Even though sometimes I do not really feel "in love" I will always be there when my lover needs me. _____

Total of all your ratings _____

A score of 23 or below indicates that you have a committed, passionate, and intimate relationship with your lover. A score between 24 and 41 falls within the average range, and suggests that certain aspects of your relationship need attention. A score above 41 suggests that your relationship suffers from weaknesses on any or all of the three dimensions—commitment, passion, or intimacy.

After summing up all your ratings, look at the total of the ratings for Items 1 through 4: the Passion Dimension. If the total for the four scales falls within the 4–8 range, give yourself a rating of "high": totals falling within the 9–14 range are average; and totals falling within the range 15–20 are low. Do the same calculations for Items 5–8 (Intimacy Dimension) and Items 9–12 (Commitment Dimension). Now circle the rating that best describe your position on each of the three dimensions:

Passion:	High	Average	Low
Intimacy:	High	Average	Low
Commitment:	High	Average	Low

After studying your partner's ratings on this scale, indicate on the five-point scale below how "compatible" you and your partner are:

1= We are totally compatible
2=We enjoy time together and share mutual interests
3=We have about an average degree of compatibility
4=We seem to have very little in common
5=We are totally incompatible

8. COMMITMENT: A high-commitment relationship generally values self-sacrifice, forgiveness of transgressions, and consistent support during times of adversity. Planning includes long-range goals; we base our relationships on patience and "being there" rather than passion or self-disclosure. When we begin to consult our friends rather than our lover, or when we begin to feel like a captive in the relationship, the term *commitment* probably isn't very accurate. The term *prisoner* might better describe our need to remain in a relationship that lacks intimacy and excitement. Here then is the Commitment Scale:

Commitment Scale

Here are ten statements that reveal the level of your commitment. Rate each statement according to the following scale:

1 = Strongly Disagree
2 = Disagree Somewhat
3 = Neither Agree nor Disagree
4 = Agree Somewhat
5 = Strongly Agree

Rating	*Item*
_____	We do not communicate as much as we did before.
_____	We're grouchy and querulous.
_____	My lover is not as available as much as I need for him/her to be.

158   Couples at the Crossroad

Rating	Item
_____	I have to compete for my lover's attention.
_____	I know it's silly, but I feel shackled to my lover.
_____	I feel clingy and "needy."
_____	I talk to outsiders about my problems more than I talk to my lover about them.
_____	I find that I worry a lot about what life will be like with my partner twenty years from now.
_____	I find that I need my lover's approval more than I want to.
_____	I feel more insecure now than I did earlier in the relationship.

Find the sum of the ratings for the ten items. Scores between 10 and 17 reflect a very strong commitment to the relationship; a score between 18 and 25 reflects a strong commitment; a score between 26 and 33 suggests an "average" commitment; a score between 34 and 41 indicates a weak commitment to the relationship; and a score between 42 and 50 suggests a totally uncommitted relationship. Circle the number on the scale below that best describes your level of commitment:

1 = Very Strongly Committed
2 = Strongly Committed
3 = Average Commitment
4 = Poorly Committed
5 = Not At All Committed

9. REASONS FOR COUPLING: Below are fifty reasons why people become involved. Rate each reason along a three-point scale. The objective is to determine whether the reason is "Very Important," "Somewhat Important" or "Not Important." Simply circle the number next to the phrase that best describes *your* motivation for becoming involved with your partner. To be fully effective, both parties should complete the scale. As you complete the scale, keep in mind that the coupling process is in large part a response to our social, emotional, financial, and sexual needs. Many attributes contribute to the probability of success: physical attraction, availability, vitality, communication, life style, intelligence, humor, intimacy, sexual attraction, and the capacity for commitment. The specific ingredients vary according to the nature of our interpersonal interactions with our

lover. With time and experience, couples develop a "we-ness" that transcends the individual traits contributed by either partner alone.

Reasons for Coupling

	Degree of Importance		
	Not Important	Important	Very Important
Intimacy	1	2	3
Sexual Attraction	1	2	3
Pity	1	2	3
Fear	1	2	3
Hero Worship	1	2	3
Mutual Interests	1	2	3
Feeling Needed	1	2	3
Feel Indebted	1	2	3
Admiration	1	2	3
Prearranged Marriage	1	2	3
Natural Thing To Do	1	2	3
Afraid to Hurt Partner	1	2	3
Desire for Family	1	2	3
Professional Growth	1	2	3
Financial Security	1	2	3
To Stop Working	1	2	3
PROPERTY	1	2	3
Reduce Taxes	1	2	3
Social Pressure	1	2	3
Leave Parents	1	2	3
Rebel Against Parents	1	2	3
To Please Parents	1	2	3

160   Couples at the Crossroad

	Degree of Importance		
	Not Important	*Important*	*Very Important*
Improve Social Life	1	2	3
Pregnancy	1	2	3
For Spite	1	2	3
Blackmail	1	2	3
Parent for Children	1	2	3
PROVE I'M NOT GAY	1	2	3
U.S. Citizenship	1	2	3
Legalize Cohabitation	1	2	3
Care for Me	1	2	3
Care for Parents	1	2	3
Loneliness	1	2	3
To Share Problems	1	2	3
To Prove I am Desirable	1	2	3
Biological Clock	1	2	3
Want to Settle Down	1	2	3
Boredom	1	2	3
On the "Rebound"	1	2	3
Spiritual Development	1	2	3
Need a Housekeeper	1	2	3
Punish Myself	1	2	3
To Experiment with Life	1	2	3
To Keep Me Young	1	2	3
To Rebuild My Life	1	2	3
Sense of Humor	1	2	3
Friendship	1	2	3
To Fend Off Enemies	1	2	3

The Decision Index   161

Degree of Importance

	Not Important	Important	Very Important
Passion	1	2	3
Commitment	1	2	3

Review your responses to these items. Circle the number on the scale below which indicates the degree to which you *share* positive motives for getting together:

1	2	3	4	5
Compatible		Somewhat Compatible		Incompatible

10. EMOTIONAL COMFORT ZONES: The emotional climate of a relationship refers to the degree to which we feel comfortable with our lover—the degree to which we can tolerate the "flat notes" of the relationship. Each couple completed the following scale:

Emotional Climate Scale

The 16 items on the scale below comprise a "thermometer" that measures the climate of your relationship. It asks you to judge how much of each personality or physical trait your partner exhibits at any particular time, and how much of each trait you find acceptable. There are two steps to the exercise:

Step 1: Place an "X" at the point on each scale that best describes how your partner behaves or presents himself.

Step 2: Underline an acceptable range for each characteristic. For example, let's rate three traits:

Emotional	1 2 3 <u>4 5 X6</u> 7	Unflappable
Serious	1 2 3 X4 <u>5 6</u> 7	Carefree
Shy	1 2 3 4 X5 <u>6 7</u>	Assertive

Here we find that the rater's partner is a fairly stable, a serious, and a somewhat shy person. What she feels most comfortable with, however, is a fairly sta-

162   Couples at the Crossroad

ble, carefree, and somewhat bold person. In two out of three cases here, her partner falls outside the "emotional comfort" zone.

Complete the following scales in a similar fashion, and answer the questions that follow in order to assess the "emotional climate" of your relationship.

Joiner	1	2	3	4	5	6	7	Loner
Relaxed	1	2	3	4	5	6	7	Driven
Impulsive	1	2	3	4	5	6	7	Controlled
Secure	1	2	3	4	5	6	7	Worried
Blunt	1	2	3	4	5	6	7	Sophisticated
Shy	1	2	3	4	5	6	7	Assertive
Self-sufficient	1	2	3	4	5	6	7	Dependent
Trusting	1	2	3	4	5	6	7	Guarded
Practical	1	2	3	4	5	6	7	Capricious
Emotional	1	2	3	4	5	6	7	Unflappable
Earthy	1	2	3	4	5	6	7	Pretentious
Serious	1	2	3	4	5	6	7	Carefree
Lackadaisical	1	2	3	4	5	6	7	Disciplined
Reserved	1	2	3	4	5	6	7	Outgoing
Casual	1	2	3	4	5	6	7	Formal
Unattractive	1	2	3	4	5	6	7	Attractive

After you have completed each item, examine the scales where your partner falls outside the emotional comfort zone. To the left of each scale where you seem to be incompatible, write an "I" (Important), an "N" (Not Important) or a "VI" (Very Important) to describe the importance of the particular characteristic. Compare the sum of the items that are rated "I"s and the items rated "VI" with the total number of "N"s. Ideally, the number of "I"s plus "VI"s should be far less than the number of "N"s.

On the scale below, circle the number that best estimates your level of emotional comfort with your lover/partner:

1 = Very High Comfort Level
2 = High Comfort Level

3 = Average Comfort Level
4 = Below Average Comfort Level
5 = Low Comfort Level

Appendix B

Four Couples at the Crossroad

Four couples completed the Decision Index scales. I later offered interpretations of each couple's profile, cautioning that this was an informal assessment. Each couple was eager to complete the Decision Index and the resultant ratings gave us a graphic picture of the relative likelihood of a successful coupling and/or the risk of failure in each of ten areas. For the purpose of this exercise, we defined a "successful coupling" as a moderately happy, stress free, exciting, committed, emotionally comforting and non-destructive relationship. First, we present a brief biography of each couple; then we offer a few observations.

Margaret and Howard

Margaret, 36-year-old woman, married an older man known for his generosity and protectiveness. When she was nine years old, she discovered that "growing up" was not allowed. Her parents took her everywhere and showered her with expensive gifts. They anticipated her every need. In turn, Margaret anticipated their need, namely, for her to be incompetent.

She decided at a young age that her parents knew best. She figured out that to be accepted by them, she had better learn to keep her opinions and feelings to herself. She found they were so protective of her that any attempt on her part to become independent produced waves of anxiety. She concluded that becoming dependent was the best way to calm them down. As an adult, she continued to play this role, maintaining a childlike existence, and looking for "parents" to protect her. Fortunately, an older gentleman expressed his willingness to take care of her, and they soon married.

Margaret discovered advantages of the little girl role. When she complained about the complexities of everyday life, her husband paid special attention to her and shouldered many of the responsibilities that rightfully belonged to her. When she complained of physical ailments, she found she could manipulate her

166   Couples at the Crossroad

husband into pampering her. Her husband, who, incidentally, went along with the game quite willingly, increased his share of the household chores. In response, Margaret favored him with sex and murmurs of appreciation. Her husband enjoyed the idea of being a hero and found that he was marching double time to the tune Margaret was playing.

After several years, however, he became resentful and disappointed. The feelings just sneaked up on him; he suddenly felt tired and weak, and he imagined the cause of his fatigue was lying in bed next to him.

Nonetheless, Margaret's husband really loved her so he tried honestly to tell her how he felt. Margaret, sensing her security slipping away, fought back by becoming "crazy" both in private and in public. Her husband redoubled his efforts, resuming his most successful role—rescuer and "parent" she tolerated the disappointment and the resentment, until finally the strain drained him of too much energy; he became less effective in business and more isolated from his friends.

When he died suddenly of congestive heart failure, people couldn't understand how such a nice man could die so young. Naturally, Margaret was overwhelmed, until, several months after her husband's death, one of his best friends, a man named Howard—also older and protective—called Margaret for a date.

By the time she and Howard came in for counseling, Margaret had become haggard and gaunt. She complained that she couldn't deal with the pressures of keeping house, caring for her two teenage sons, and be a good wife to Howard. For a long while, Howard responded—as did his predecessor—with compassion and offers of relief. It occurred to him after a particularly harrowing day that he too was tired and simply worn out trying to keep up with Margaret's various ailments.

Margaret learned her helpless role well. She spent much of her time listing the many things that made her feel small and unprotected. Everyday responsibilities overwhelmed her. Asked what she could do to remedy the situation, she dropped her head to her chest and became mute. In the meantime, people around her, friends, in-laws, Howard, and her two sons, faced daily with Margaret's unhappy expression, protected her and assumed responsibility for her work at home.

Turning our attention to Howard, we found that he was an "impostor." He had decided early on that he was small and inadequate. His lack of self-esteem required that he (and everyone else in the world) see him as the commander-and-chief, decision-maker, wheeler-dealer, and head honcho in his relationships. In reality, he was less bright and capable than his than Margaret, who, during the earlier part of the marriage, paid the bills and pumped up Howard's ego. In fact,

Howard's modest success in business was due in large part to Margaret's industriousness and creativity. Howard knew—or at least sensed—that he was less competent than Margaret. With this vague awareness came the twin emotions of guilt and resentment.

For nearly eight years, he accepted his Margaret's judgments, but he made it perfectly clear that he was still the boss. Margaret, of course, was delighted to hear that; it fit in nicely with her need to be secure and protected by someone bigger and stronger than she was. Howard's belief that marriage was an equal partnership with the wife just slightly less equal than the husband did not bother Margaret at all.

After several counseling sessions, I asked Margaret and Howard to complete the ten scales on the Decision Index. You'll find the results on a Decision Index Table below. The ♀ sign represents the wife's scores on the various scales. It reflects her *perception* of her husband or their relationship. The ♂ represents the male's score on a particular scale and his *perception* of his wife or their relationship. For example, if a husband (♂) were to rate his wife (♀) as a "4" on the Burden scale, we would interpret that to mean that he perceives his wife to be frequently overwhelmed by emotional, medical or financial stress. Likewise, if a wife's score (♀) on the Destructiveness Scale was "5," it would suggest that either or both members of the couple have done irreparable harm to the relationship because of the destructive behavior/attitudes. In this regard, if a wife's score on the Destructiveness Scale was "1," but she has been seen in the emergency room on numerous occasions because of physical trauma, we would suspect that the wife is denying a very blatant and a very damaging reality. With this in mind, let's see how Margaret and Howard rated the ten decision making factors as depicted in the following table. Note: Higher numbers suggest a greater likelihood of failure.

Decision Index
Likelihood of Successful Coupling
Howard & Margaret

	5 (very poor)	4	3 (average)	2	1 (excellent)
7-Signs of Love		♂	♀		
Burden	♂			♀	
Trainer		♂		♀	
Bonding		♂	♀		
Rapport			♂ ♀		
Destructive Behavior	♂			♀	
PIC Compatibility		♂	♀		
Commitment		♂		♀	
Reasons Coupling			♂ ♀		
Emotional Comfort		♂	♀		

Immediately we see some obvious differences. Howard (♂) rated 7 of the 10 attributes within the high risk of failure range. He sees Margaret (♀) as an overwhelmed woman whose parents trained her to be compliant but clingy and emotionally aloof. He feels that he and Margaret are not committed to the marriage, his ratings suggesting long periods of bickering followed expressions of insecurity. The poor quality of sex, the endless arguments about minor matters and Margaret's temper outbursts raised the scores on the Destructive Behavior and Attitude scale. Margaret's moodiness, her alternating periods of tension and impulsivity mixed with insecurity, produced an irritability and impatience in Howard that even he admitted were less than admirable.

Margaret's ratings are even more interesting. All of her scores fell at a "3" level or below. She did not feel that Howard was particularly unhappy. In her view, he was not overwhelmed by stress, he showed three or four love signs, and she felt that they were both relatively committed to the marriage. According to her ratings, there were no particular problems with destructive behavior and they were relatively compatible in terms of passion, intimacy and commitment.

How can a relationship like this possibly succeed? Howard and Margaret seemed to be living in two different realities. Margaret was denying the very real

Four Couples at the Crossroad   169

problems in her marriage, and Howard was stuck with her because of his own need for someone who refused to see the flaws in his personality.

The outcome? After innumerable separations and reconciliations, the couple split up. Of course, Howard moved across the street so he could be available to Margaret if she should ever need anything—sex included. On her part, Margaret continued to believe they would get back together someday; boys would be boys after all, and once that "middle-age crisis thingee" was over, she was sure Howard would come back. She might be right. I would not have bet on it. It would depend on Howard's very substantial level of guilt, his need to be admired as a wheeler-dealer, and Margaret's ability to maneuver him into believing that *now* she was *totally* helpless.

Susan and Dennis

Susan was a beautiful 26-year-old single woman who drew the attention of both men and women. She was pretty enough to be a top model earning an income in six figures. The most eligible bachelors sought her out and, on occasion, some of the most eligible bachelorettes sought her out as well. She discovered early in her teens that people responded only to her face, not her mind. She decided she was never going to be able to earn respect as an ordinary person, so she honed her ability to seduce people with her considerable charm and sensuality.

Behind all the manipulations and seductions, Susan felt angry and resentful about the lack of appreciation and respect. She entertained a stream of both men and women who thought they could successfully maneuver her into bed. Unable to express her frustration and resentment directly, she provoked them, promising them excitement and good times, and then failed to deliver the goodies (herself). Occasionally, she did find someone who would sweep her off her feet, but the encounters were short-lived.

Despite her facial beauty, she did not really feel very good about herself; she did not really understand what people saw in her. She felt superficial and ugly, and when she looked in the mirror, she saw only her blemishes and none of her true beauty. She discounted compliments and relegated them to the "insincere" pile.

She experienced little pleasure from human contact, complaining bitterly that men just couldn't turn her on sexually. She tried to make contact with others—men or women—by provoking them with her stubbornness, sexiness, and dramatics. When her escorts of either sex responded in kind, Susan became outraged. Her escorts ended up feeling confused and angry.

170   Couples at the Crossroad

Susan's father, a man who could make his daughter giggle and coo, died before Susan could swallow and digest his words of comfort. The upshot was that Susan walked around distrusting everyone; she was sensitive and defensive, and she earned a reputation for being irritable and grouchy. The voices dominating her life are those of her never-satisfied mother and a frightened, threatened, angry little girl who lost her playfulness and spontaneity when she was merely three years old.

When Susan reached 25, she decided it was time to have a family. She told her friends she was going to "snag" a guy within the next six months. Four months later, she found someone who she thought was a little less noxious than most of the guys she'd dated. The man's name was Dennis.

Dennis was a 32-year-old divorced father of three. He readily admitted that emotionally he was still an 18 year old, but he did not really believe it. (Everybody else did.) He spent his entire adult life chasing after and capturing the hearts of women. He was searching, he told me, for the perfect "10." When he met Susan at a party, he thought she was the most beautiful woman he'd ever seen, and the rest—as they say—is history.

Dennis decided at an early age that he would emulate Broadway Joe Namath (New York Jets Quarterback), one of the few real men around. H e liked Joe's style, his sense of humor, his confidence, and most of all his legendary skill as a lothario.

Dennis' mother was a hard working, totally caring woman who, of her three children, selected Dennis as "special." She never said "No" to him, readily gave in to his wishes, and protected him from adversity. So deeply did she feel for him, she (and the other children) went without essentials to provide him with the best clothing and the not-always-affordable little red sports car. Dennis' father did not always agree with his wife, but he felt he couldn't go against her wishes without arousing her ire. Neither parent ever questioned Dennis' feelings and judgments. Eventually, without the appropriate reality checks offered by mature parents, he came to believe the fantasies offered by magazines and television were what life was really about.

For the most part, Dennis' relationships were disastrous. While his girlfriends were often terrific companions in public, there seemed to be something missing in the relationship. Some women could contribute nothing to a conversation other than gossipy appraisals of various entertainers: Others proved too bright, too perceptive and too explosive, not at all the kind of unconditional adoration Dennis was used to. Many women initially enjoyed Dennis' attention. The "10" types to which he was attracted enjoyed being shown off to his friends; like

Susan, they thoroughly enjoyed seducing him, manipulating him into making promises both he and they knew he couldn't keep. And then they lowered the boom! The mutually satisfying seduction phase of these relationships invariably wore thin after the first few dates. Dennis couldn't deliver the glamour and excitement he promised, and his dates became sulky and resentful.

Let's take a look at Dennis' (♂) and Susan's (♀) profiles:

Decision Index
Likelihood of Successful Coupling
Dennis & Susan

	5	4	3	2	1
7-Signs of Love		♀ ♂			
Burden		♀	♂		
Trainer		♀ ♂			
Bonding	♀		♂		
Rapport	♀	♂			
Destructive Behavior	♂		♀		
PIC Compatibility		♀ ♂			
Commitment	♀ ♂				
Reasons Coupling		♂	♀		
Emotional Comfort		♀ ♂			

5	4	3	2	1
(very poor)		(average)		(excellent)

What is there to say about this profile! How could two people who differ so much even bother to date, let alone get married? Looking at their profiles, you can readily understand why there might be difficulties in the marriage. Of the seven "signs" of love, they could count only three. The major "sign" was possessiveness. But it was extreme. Susan was threatened by any female who she felt might compete with her for Dennis' affections. Dennis was extremely jealous of other men whom Susan had chosen to flirt with.

On the Destructive Behavior and Attitude Scale they both displayed physical aggression, in one instance requiring a brief visit to the local hospital for Dennis who'd been cut by broken glass. They both displayed temper outbursts, smashing furniture, breaking dishes, and tearing clothing. Sexual activity, a major strength

172 Couples at the Crossroad

in the relationship, had ceased entirely by the time they came in for marital therapy.

In addition, each felt that the "training" the other had got as a child was lacking. Dennis' ratings placed Susan at the high-risk level, reflecting his belief that she did not get the right kind of discipline at home. Her father died when she was a toddler, and her mother simply couldn't handle a bright, pretty, and manipulative little girl. Mother accepted all behaviors, good and bad, and reinforced Susan's need to be dramatic and demanding. Susan perceived Dennis as a spoiled bratty child who had grown up to be a spoiled bratty adult. He was unreliable, and he could neither bond nor develop a meaningful sense of intimacy and commitment. Dennis, on the other hand, saw Susan as an incorrigible, manipulative, extremely intense woman who—if the truth be told—frightened him with her temper tantrums and constant criticism. The marriage lasted about three months before one of Susan's friends suggested that an annulment might be a good idea. Interestingly enough, as soon as the need for cooperative and mature behavior ended, Dennis and Susan began dating. Sex was satisfying; and the destructive behaviors they displayed during the marriage subsided. Susan put her desire for a family on hold. Dennis continued to look for a "10" at the local watering hole, and when he became too lonely he would call Susan who, depending on her availability, would entertain Dennis for the evening.

Given the brevity of their relationship, it would appear that Susan and Dennis' life scripts were incompatible. But at a deeper level, they were not: Dennis found Susan, and Susan made herself found, because all parties involved need an excuse to avoid intimacy. "Incompatible" life scripts serve this purpose admirably. While all parties appeared to be resentful, angry, hurt, etc., the termination of each relationship actually brought relief to all the people involved. When the two people had met, they were struggling with a major decision: Should they or shouldn't they give up their most precious possession—their egos.

Angela and Jim

When Angela was a teenager, she decided she had a weight problem. The real problem was that she had lost control of her physical and psychological boundaries long before her teens. She could not say *no* to anything. She accepted food, criticism, and compliments with equal fervor, never wanting to alienate anyone or risk abandonment by them. The result was overeating, over-talking, overdrinking, and over-complaining. To maintain her boundaries she tried diet after diet, hoping that somehow this would prevent her from abusing herself and other people. She would tell you she simply wants to feel good about herself—that she wanted to gain the acceptance of the people around her.

As a child, her mother told her to eat everything on her plate. She was not allowed to refuse a second helping at dinner time because, said her mother, "Children all over the world are starving" Angela became obsessed with food as a teenager, and her parents, forgetting how they fostered the weight gain to begin with, sent her to a special camp for overweight girls. In doing so, they sent her a clear message: Now she was not acceptable even to them!

Angela's inability to say "No" generalized to other aspects of her life. She was not able to say "No" to anything. She devoured criticism and compliments as readily as any dessert. She was unable to express anger or resentment, because actually this too would be like saying "No." She had also discovered that her obesity gave her a certain advantage: She no longer had to deal with the issue of intimacy with men. Ironically, while she felt weak and small inside, her vast bulk made her feel substantial and solid.

As a young girl, Angela chose Oprah as a model. Whenever the talented talk show host went on a diet, Angela did also. Whenever Oprah changed her hairstyle or her style of dress, Angela saved money until she could buy clothing that matched—in size, if not in quality. Eventually, she recognized there was a serious problem and she joined Overeaters Anonymous, and there she met Jim.

Jim was a 38-year-old career soldier. His father, a retired Master Sergeant in the Marine Corps, was his idol. They spent much time together when Jim was young, father always reminding his son that men and women were different. The main difference, he said, was "You can never trust a woman." Father also implied you could never trust anyone else either, but women, in his view, were particularly evil.

Jim observed his parents closely after this revelation, and after a period of years, he discovered that his father really did not trust women—especially Jim's mother. But Jim couldn't understand why: She gave everything she had to her children—Jim, his brother and his two sisters. She cleaned and cooked, and washed their clothes. She read bedtime stories to them and bandaged their cuts and scrapes.

No matter: Jim believed his father. He did not discern the Master Sergeant's basic paranoid posture.

Jim's favorite movie was Patton with George C. Scott in the lead role. He learned that ruthlessness, obstinacy, pride, glory and courage in the face of danger were the most important ingredients in any real man's life. Jim joined the service immediately after graduating from High School. He remained a bachelor, spend-

174   Couples at the Crossroad

ing most of his available time in the pursuit of all-male activities. For sexual release, Jim was quite comfortable visiting a brothel near the base.

As Jim became older, he became increasingly bitter. His friends, he felt, had abandoned him by getting married and settling into decidedly un-masculine roles of obedient husbands and fathers. Jim felt out of place and he felt awkward.

His bitterness grew. He felt alone and empty. Neither his father nor Patton had prepared him for this!

He discovered through these experiences that his father was correct: He could trust neither men nor women. Prior to meeting Angela at an OA meeting, Jim had been engaged. Shortly before the wedding date, however, the injunctions Jim learned about intimacy, passion, and commitment took control and he backed out of the marriage, leaving a hurt and perplexed almost-bride-to-be trying to figure out what had gone wrong.

Fear of deception and betrayal compromised Jim's judgment. As his suspicions grew, so did his penchant for building a case against people, not just women but men as well. Nurturing behavior on the part of others was simply unacceptable.

Jim married Angela at the urging of his mother who desperately wanted grandchildren. Angela of course accepted Jim with all his faults. He was critical, disrespectful, and mean, especially when drunk, a relatively common occurrence since he spent a substantial portion of his monthly allotments at the local tavern. Here is the profile Angela (♀) and Jim (♂) produced:

Decision Index
Likelihood of Successful Coupling
Jim & Angela

	5	4	3	2	1
7-Signs of Love		♂			♀
Burden	♂		♀		
Trainer		♀ ♂			
Bonding		♂		♀	
Rapport		♂		♀	
Destructive Behavior			♂	♀	
PIC Compatibility	♂				♀
Commitment	♂			♀	
Reasons Coupling		♂		♀	
Emotional Comfort			♂ ♀		

5	4	3	2	1
(very poor)		(average)		(excellent)

The profile is exactly what we might expect: Angela still couldn't say "No" and Jim apparently couldn't say "Yes." Angela denied any serious problems in the relationship. In her eyes, Jim showed all the signs of love—even when he was drunk and batting her around! She did not see him as particularly burdened, although his drinking and eating habits placed him at-risk for heart problems and a variety of other medically related illnesses. She felt he was a committed, intimate, passionate man whose reasons for marrying her might be different from her reasons, but so what! She simply loved the guy. She viewed him as a man who was just misunderstood by most people. When you got to know him, she thought, he was really a deep thinker. Rapport between them was great, and, despite the fact that he had whacked her a few times, and that they were constantly bickering about politics and values, she did not see any major destructive behaviors or attitudes.

Of course, Jim's take on the marriage was different. In his view, Angela was an overwhelmed, dependent woman who on the surface would have liked you to believe she was caring, protective, and generous with her attention. But he knew that underneath it all, she was just like all the other women he'd been with: clingy, uncommitted, and unable to relate to him in a way that really made sense. His profile suggested that he was desperately unhappy with Angela; Angela's profile suggested that she was desperately happy with Jim. The only thing they seemed to have in common was a degree of desperation, a constant need for companionship without intimacy.

How did this marriage turn out? Angela and Jim celebrated their 35th wedding anniversary in 1999. They have four grown children: Two are reasonably successful in their respective marriages, and two have entered the military service so they can be hero-warriors like their dad. (At least that's the way their mother described him!) The case reinforces what most of us already know: alcohol and denial can overcome virtually all problems (but the side effects might kill you).

Lisa and Billy

Lisa, a 34-year-old blonde flight attendant, was proud of her self-sufficiency and independence. She established her existential position early in life when she discovered that neither her mother, an alcoholic, nor her father, overwhelmed by the challenge of an alcoholic wife, were available to her and her siblings. She learned that at the age of seven it was safer not to depend on others because invariably they let her down.

176   Couples at the Crossroad

Asked what she remembers most about her childhood, she will tell you about the great movies she saw on television. She especially enjoyed watching movies that featured "tough" ladies like Bette Davis and Katherine Hepburn. If you press her, she recalls how she and her family were always in the midst of a crisis. Because her mother drank and her father was in and out of the hospital for treatment of depression, Lisa and her brothers and sisters—there were six in all—were told not to reveal anything about the family's affairs. Her mother made it clear it was "us against the world."

Survival depended on learning how to be tough and self-reliant. After years of programming by her mother, Lisa finally figured out she couldn't trust anyone: She decided she would have to compete and battle for everything she got. She also learned to suppress feelings of tenderness and any of the emotions that might be mistaken for weakness.

Bright and witty, Lisa took great delight putting down people—men and women alike—for their lack of courage and aggressiveness. Men regarded her as "castrating" by, and women saw her as "bitchy." Many people appreciated her gutsy attitude, but as the years passed, she discovered that few people could tolerate her judgmental attitude.

Occasionally, she dated men who, at first, seemed to enjoy her insightful if somewhat cynical perceptions of the social scene. After several weeks, however, Lisa, feeling seduced and frightened by contact with tender and dependent feelings, put on the brakes, terminated the relationship, and withdrew into a shell until the danger of vulnerability passed.

None of Lisa's dates had ever seen her profound sense of compassion or even suspected that she volunteered at the local hospice comforting terminally ill patients and their families. What they remembered most about their experience with her was the vague sense of her distrust; she seemed to go out of her way to catch people doing something wrong, and then to thoroughly enjoy cutting their legs from under them. It seemed to them that Lisa's goal was to prove she was better than everybody else.

She ended up feeling lonely and cynical. She thought she might have found a cure for this emotional dyspepsia when she met a man named Bill at one of the posh singles bars.

William (his parents call him Billy) was a handsome 42-year-old man who decided at the age of 14 that maleness and athletic accomplishment were the same. He took a Charles Atlas muscle builder course, lifted weights with his friends, and tried out successfully for varsity sports. He prided himself on being one of the few three-letter men in school.

Four Couples at the Crossroad   177

Five nights a week, you could find him on the basketball court practicing with semi-pro team. Every morning, before work, you could find him in the gym, building and rebuilding his body, defining his muscles, looking spiffy in his black spandex trunks. It seemed that he would rather be in the gym than be with a girl, an irony since one of the reasons he gives for working out so often was that he wanted to make himself more attractive.

As Billy grew into his twenties, he discovered that most women responded better to gentle words than to hardened muscle. Since he had no gentle words—or gentle thoughts for that matter—he began to feel isolated and unappreciated. Overwhelmed by isolation, exacerbated by the fact that most of his friends were married, he began to drink large quantities of alcohol and to eat even larger quantities of food. At home (he still lived with Mom and Dad), he spent many hours watching sporting events on television, reminiscing with his father about "the good old days" when he was able to run the hundred-yard dash in 9.4 seconds. His dates—the few he had—often complained that he could not talk about current events or anything else not related to macho things.

Billy's father always emphasized the competitive aspects of any encounter. There always had to be a winner, he would tell Billy, often while the two were working on a fifth of Bourbon during half time. They enjoyed putting "egg heads" down, because "they had no common sense" even if they could make money.

Billy accepted these attributions as real, never questioning his father's observations. It was not until Bill Bradley, a basketball star who later became a politician, extolled the virtues of intelligence that Billy became even dimly aware that his interest in athletics was not antithetical to reading a book from the New York Times best seller's list. When he told his father he had decided to take night courses at the local college, Dad was not impressed. Fortunately, his mother was; she encouraged him through words and careful attention to continue to build his mind with the same vigor with which he built his body. Billy stuck with it until he earned an Associate's Degree.

He also stuck with a diet of good food. Finally, he joined Alcoholics Anonymous. This left his father sitting alone in front of the television on many a night. Billy felt a bit guilty about this, but his guilt abated once he met Lisa who seemed to appreciate Billy's efforts and who had rediscovered in herself a depth of compassion she had buried long ago. Nonetheless, the two people were struggling. At times, it was not easy. A review of their profiles reveals why.

Decision Index
Likelihood of Successful Coupling
Billy & Lisa

	5	4	3	2	1
7-Signs of Love			♀	♂	
Burden			♀	♂	
Trainer	♂		♀		
Bonding	♂			♀	
Rapport				♂ ♀	
Destructive Behavior			♀	♂	
PIC Compatibility	♀			♂	
Commitment				♀	♂
Reasons Coupling				♂ ♀	
Emotional Comfort			♀	♂	
	5 (very poor)	**4**	**3** (average)	**2**	**1** (excellent)

Bill's profile tells us that he had developed a passion and a commitment for his marriage. He perceived their relationship as complete: The signs of love and compatibility were there—at least for him. He felt their reasons for coupling were healthy, and further that they really enjoyed being with each other. There were some minor problems, he admitted, especially in the area of bonding and training. He recognized that her childhood was not a happy one, that both of her parents had major issues with alcohol or emotional stress. She was "trained" by an impersonal environment and she had trouble accepting Bill's love for her. Bonding was particularly difficult, Bill often throwing up his hands and wondering whether it was all worth it. Yet, in Bill's eyes, Lisa was simply superb. Denial is a particularly powerful defense against bad thoughts.

Lisa did not see it quite the same way. She recognized that Bill loved her in his own fashion, but felt that Bill could not relate as deeply as she needed him to. What she failed to appreciate was that her concern reflected her *own* inability to develop intimacy. She believed Bill was under a lot of stress and that his parents, like hers, had provided little except the essentials—shelter, clothing, food. In her view, his pre-occupation with his body was his way of warding off bad thoughts and bad feelings—at least that was the way *she* helped get rid of *her* own bad thoughts and bad feelings. Fortunately, as her ratings showed, she did get a sense that the two were compatible in the most important areas: passion, commitment, intimacy, reasons for coupling, and emotional comfort.

What could counseling do in a situation like this? At first I thought the state of affairs was hopeless. Then I saw the profiles and changed my mind. Lisa and Bill, despite neglectful or emotionally difficult childhoods, had something many couples seeking counseling did not have: They had goodwill, courage, and enough resilience to work through their difficulties. With time, Lisa became more trusting; Bill matured, continued attending the meetings at AA, and eventually graduated from a Bachelor's program at one of the Boston's major universities.

Who would have guessed? Both people were untrusting, suspicious, and often showed disdain for both men and women. Yet, despite this, Lisa and Bill had managed to find what Mike and Ann had finally found—the path with the heart. The last I heard, Lisa was pregnant with her second child; Bill had established a small business in town. They still send a Christmas card every year.

A Personal Note

Behind every number on every graph there is a reality, often hidden, often at odds with what we feel to be true. The fact is that we still don't know what makes people tick, nor do we know how couples manage to stay together despite the evidence of monumental emotional struggle. We have noted earlier that two "weak" characters can produce a strong union, while two "strong" characters who can't learn to share their egos, physical space, and emotional space are likely to end up in divorce court. We often can't predict what will happen to people over the long haul.

Sometimes the scales and concepts we use to help people work well; sometimes they do not, depending on the honesty of the informants, the circumstances that bring them into the consultation room and our own sensitivity to the needs of the client. These facts notwithstanding, men and women who understand the roles of early childhood upbringing, mood sequences, destructive habits and thoughts, parental injunctions and attributions, life scripts, toxic personalities, fantasy, and the many faces of "compatibility" will reduce the probability of making poor decisions at any of the three stages of coupling. Making choices at the crossroad is always difficult. I hope *Couples at the Crossroad—Finding the Path with a Heart* will make the task easier.

Index

A

Acts of Destruction 85

Addiction 9, 77, 78

Androgyny 30

Anger

    Disgust 68, 69, 70, 83, 85

    Resentment 48, 54, 65, 68, 69, 70, 81, 85, 99, 127, 166, 167, 169, 173

    Vindictiveness 23, 68, 69, 70, 81, 85

    Withdrawal 8, 10, 16, 36, 46, 48, 59, 68, 69, 70, 76, 78, 79, 81, 82, 83, 85, 117, 118

Assuming Control 87

Awareness 13, 16, 30, 67, 72, 74, 77, 87, 109, 110, 111, 112, 113, 114, 115, 116, 118, 122, 127, 133, 135, 140, 150, 167

Awareness Exercises

    Becoming You/Becoming Me 116

    Contact/Withdrawal 117

    Create-A-Product 119

    Expanding Boundaries 136

    Fears/Wishes 130

    Finger-Pointing 33, 122

    Have To/Choose To 127, 128

    Make-A-Sandwich 133

    Yes/No 124

B

Bonding 7, 8, 11, 12, 18, 21, 152, 153, 178

Burden 9, 11, 12, 46, 91, 144, 152, 167

C

Castenada, Carlos xi

Comfort Zones 23, 24, 161

Commitment xii, 4, 5, 6, 7, 9, 11, 14, 15, 16, 17, 18, 20, 27, 32, 40, 52, 54, 57, 60, 63, 64, 65, 66, 81, 100, 107, 108, 109, 150, 155, 156, 157, 158, 161, 168, 172, 174, 178, 179

Compatibility 14, 15, 16, 19, 65, 72, 107, 111, 155, 157, 178, 179

Confusion 16, 40, 79, 86, 109, 115, 119, 127

Connecting 8, 51, 61, 107

Contact Boundaries 58, 59, 87, 135, 136

Couplehood 5, 53

Couples xi, xii, xiii, 4, 6, 8, 14, 16, 19, 23, 30, 54, 55, 56, 59, 76, 94, 108, 120, 151, 156, 159, 165, 179

Coupling xii, xiii, 5, 6, 14, 16, 17, 18, 20, 21, 31, 32, 51, 52, 54, 55, 56, 57, 63, 64, 84, 86, 107, 108, 109, 134, 158, 159, 165, 178, 179

Courage 37, 68, 81, 107, 108, 173, 176, 179

Critical Parent 31, 33, 34, 36, 44, 109, 124, 133, 152

D

Decision Index 15, 21, 24, 65, 151, 165, 167

Demands xii, 8, 31, 33, 34, 46, 51, 68, 73, 97, 98, 99, 109, 112, 122, 123, 124, 125, 127, 130

Depression 8, 10, 23, 61, 68, 69, 76, 95, 111, 176

Destructive Attitudes and Behaviors 21, 153

Discouragement 10, 68

Do's and Don'ts 97

Dreams

    Dreams as Existential Messages 145

182 Couples at the Crossroad

Dreams as Part of the Grieving Process 142
Dreams as Unfinished Business 139, 140
Dreams-Then and Now 139

E

Early Decisions 81, 95, 97, 98, 99, 101
Emotional Climate 23, 24, 25, 26, 27, 40, 42, 45, 46, 47, 48, 51, 54, 108, 161, 162
Emotional Death 85
Emotional Withdrawal 10, 16, 48
Eros 29, 30
Existential Positions 95, 98

F

Failure xii, 10, 11, 61, 76, 77, 78, 79, 81, 84, 96, 119, 140, 151, 165, 166, 167, 168
Fantasy 4, 57, 59, 112, 113, 114, 117, 118, 119, 122, 137, 144, 179
Fatigue 10, 69, 166
Fear 10, 17, 23, 32, 35, 48, 59, 60, 62, 64, 70, 79, 80, 125, 128, 130, 132, 133, 138, 139, 140, 159, 174
Feelings xii, 5, 6, 7, 8, 10, 15, 17, 23, 26, 31, 33, 34, 35, 36, 38, 41, 42, 48, 52, 53, 54, 55, 56, 57, 58, 59, 60, 61, 62, 64, 66, 68, 69, 70, 71, 72, 73, 74, 76, 78, 80, 81, 83, 84, 85, 86, 87, 96, 98, 99, 100, 107, 108, 109, 110, 111, 112, 117, 119, 122, 123, 124, 125, 126, 127, 128, 129, 131, 132, 133, 137, 138, 139, 140, 147, 151, 152, 155, 156, 165, 166, 170, 176, 178
Flow of Emotions 82, 84
Folié Á Deux 6, 18
Frustration 10, 16, 31, 46, 70, 71, 77, 78, 79, 80, 81, 84, 100, 169

H

Happiness xii, 5, 14, 16, 34, 47, 55, 58, 64, 77, 78, 98, 100, 101, 112, 124, 140
Heroes 77, 97, 98, 100
Hidden Realities 107
Honesty xii, 40, 57, 83, 121, 179

Hopelessness 10, 70, 71, 80
Humiliation 33, 70, 71, 72, 74, 80, 81, 83, 84

I

Infatuation 4, 112
Intimacy xii, 4, 5, 6, 7, 8, 9, 10, 11, 12, 14, 15, 16, 17, 18, 20, 27, 29, 30, 40, 45, 46, 52, 53, 54, 56, 57, 58, 59, 60, 61, 62, 64, 65, 66, 76, 77, 86, 93, 100, 108, 119, 127, 135, 148, 150, 153, 155, 156, 157, 158, 159, 168, 172, 173, 174, 175, 178, 179
Intrusion and Abandonment 59
Irritability 10, 38, 60, 96, 111, 168
Isolation 58, 70, 71, 74, 76, 80, 118, 177

L

Life Scripts xii, xiii, 16, 52, 67, 94, 95, 97, 98, 101, 108, 172, 179
Loss of Control 6, 10, 57, 96, 100
Love v, xi, xii, 4, 5, 6, 7, 9, 10, 14, 16, 17, 20, 29, 30, 31, 32, 34, 37, 39, 40, 41, 44, 45, 46, 47, 51, 52, 53, 54, 55, 56, 59, 60, 61, 63, 64, 65, 71, 73, 75, 76, 77, 78, 79, 80, 83, 85, 86, 89, 99, 100, 107, 116, 124, 126, 127, 129, 131, 132, 135, 140, 144, 148, 149, 150, 151, 152, 155, 156, 168, 171, 175, 178
Lying 8, 138, 148, 149, 166

M

Moments of Truth 108, 134
Moods 52, 67, 68, 77, 79, 81, 82, 83, 84, 85, 86, 107
Motivation for Coupling 16, 20, 51

N

Nature of Awareness 110
Nurturing Parent 152

O

Ownership 9, 11, 12, 51, 53

Index 183

P

Paradox of Change 109

Passion xii, 4, 5, 6, 7, 9, 11, 14, 15, 16, 17, 18, 20, 27, 29, 30, 31, 32, 34, 36, 40, 53, 54, 55, 57, 60, 64, 65, 66, 77, 108, 150, 155, 156, 157, 161, 168, 174, 178, 179

Past Performances 11

Path with a Heart xi, xiii, 15, 88, 149, 179

Phantom Pains 74, 75

Philia 29

Plato 30

Possessor 48

Power of Moods 67

R

Rapport 7, 11, 12, 21, 153, 175

Realities xii, 3, 31, 61, 107, 118, 168

Rejection 21, 36, 41, 46, 52, 64, 74, 76, 85, 148

Relationship xii, 3, 4, 5, 6, 7, 9, 10, 11, 12, 14, 15, 16, 17, 18, 19, 20, 22, 23, 24, 25, 26, 27, 32, 33, 34, 36, 37, 40, 41, 44, 45, 46, 47, 48, 51, 52, 53, 54, 55, 56, 57, 59, 60, 61, 63, 64, 65, 66, 67, 68, 69, 71, 72, 74, 75, 76, 77, 78, 84, 85, 87, 92, 93, 95, 98, 100, 101, 102, 107, 108, 109, 113, 117, 118, 119, 122, 125, 126, 127, 130, 133, 134, 139, 148, 150, 151, 153, 154, 155, 156, 157, 158, 161, 162, 165, 167, 168, 170, 172, 175, 176, 178

Resentment 48, 54, 65, 68, 69, 70, 81, 85, 99, 127, 166, 167, 169, 173

Resonance Factor 19

Roles xii, 56, 82, 90, 91, 95, 99, 125, 174, 179

S

Scripts Lovers Live

    Early Decisions 81, 95, 97, 98, 99, 101

    Life Script Exercises 101

    Life Script Heroes 97

Secret Fears, Secret Desires 105

Self-Reliance 8

Seven Signs of Love

    Balance 26, 32, 36, 39, 44, 45, 52, 53, 54, 55, 56, 64, 78, 79, 100, 101, 108, 118, 127, 129, 152

    Exclusive Companionship 52, 151

    Feelings of Safety 8

    Possessiveness 12, 44, 48, 53, 152, 171

    Sex 10, 21, 22, 29, 30, 54, 55, 132, 140, 141, 152, 154, 166, 168, 169, 172

    Shared Thoughts 55

    Trust 8, 22, 37, 52, 57, 59, 63, 66, 71, 95, 101, 107, 133, 135, 152, 154, 173, 174, 176

Spontaneous Child 31

Stability 19, 65, 108, 155

Stage I Contact 1

Stage II Connection 49

Stage III Secret Fears, Secret Desires 105

Stamina 19, 74, 82, 108, 145

Symmetry 19

T

Three Dimensions of Love

    Commitment xii, 4, 5, 6, 7, 9, 11, 14, 15, 16, 17, 18, 20, 27, 32, 40, 52, 54, 57, 60, 63, 64, 65, 66, 81, 100, 107, 108, 109, 150, 155, 156, 157, 158, 161, 168, 172, 174, 178, 179

    Intimacy xii, 4, 5, 6, 7, 8, 9, 10, 11, 12, 14, 15, 16, 17, 18, 20, 27, 29, 30, 40, 45, 46, 52, 53, 54, 56, 57, 58, 59, 60, 61, 62, 64, 65, 66, 76, 77, 86, 93, 100, 108, 119, 127, 135, 148, 150, 153, 155, 156, 157, 158, 159, 168, 172, 173, 174, 175, 178, 179

    Passion xii, 4, 5, 6, 7, 9, 11, 14, 15, 16, 17, 18, 20, 27, 29, 30, 31, 32, 34, 36, 40, 53, 54, 55, 57, 60, 64, 65, 66, 77, 108, 150, 155, 156, 157, 161, 168, 174, 178, 179

Three Little Pigs 32

Three Spheres of Awareness 111, 113

Toxic Personalities
The "Double-Binder" 46
The "Whiner" 47
The Armadillo 47
The IFTFA PERSON 47
The IFTFA Person 46
The Impulsive Thinker 43, 44, 45
The Non-Thinker 41, 45
The Obsessive Thinker 37, 38, 39, 40, 41, 42, 44, 45, 48
The Suspicious Thinker 39, 40, 41, 44, 48
The Trapper 45
Trainers 51

V

Values xii, 15, 16, 18, 19, 21, 22, 55, 57, 72, 88, 99, 108, 120, 150, 154, 157, 175

W

Wishes xii, 18, 30, 38, 41, 51, 126, 130, 131, 132, 133, 145, 170

Z

Zeus 30

0-595-29657-2

LaVergne, TN USA
20 October 2010
201638LV00002B/1/A